Hearts, Tarts & RASCALS
The Story of Bettys

Copyright © Jonathan Wild, 2005
First published in Great Britain in 2005
Second edition published in Great Britain in 2010
by Bettys & Taylors Group,
1 Parliament Street,
Harrogate HG1 2QU

Jonathan Wild asserts the moral right to be identified as the author of this work
in accordance with the Copyright, Designs & Patents Act, 1988.

Edited by Sarah McKee and Dom Dwight.

Designed by Georgina Gill, Rebecca Watson, and Laura Jukes.

Printed by Team (Impression) Limited, Leeds.

ISBN 978-0-9550914-2-1

Contents

Introduction

'Bettys is a rich infusion of past and present which you drink down with your tea, knowing that it is the very essence of Englishness' *Phil Smith – writer and broadcaster*

This is the story of Bettys, past and present, from the perspective of the founding family's third generation.

Others would tell it differently, especially my father, Victor Wild, on whose collection of family letters and diaries this book is based. However, it is my hand that is holding the pen, and this is a very personal account, a scrapbook of memories and anecdotes rather than a complete history.

My wife, Lesley, and me in our vegetable garden

After thirty-five years working in the family business with the last fifteen as its leader, I ought to be able to tell you everything about Bettys. That the family cannot in all truth answer the simple question 'Who was Betty?' indicates that some of the gaps between the facts – spaces where true history lies – are not just intriguing, they are downright mystifying. You would expect more precision from a Swiss family; or perhaps, like me, you prefer a good mystery.

For all our Englishness, we are in fact an immigrant family, from that generation of young Swiss hopefuls, like Caesar Ritz, who journeyed, penniless, to the heart of the British Empire in search of fame and fortune. In the course of this story our founder, Fritz Bützer, becomes almost more English than the English. The young 'Fritz' transforms himself into 'Frederick' as he builds his business. Now the successful entrepreneur, he becomes 'Dickie' to his friends. As head of a family dynasty he becomes simply 'Uncle'. *'In my heart I am still the same old Fritz'*, he once wrote to my grandmother.

This second printing of 'Hearts, Tarts & Rascals' is dedicated to my wife, Lesley. We have worked together at Bettys for over thirty years and early in 2009 she took over from me as Chairman – the third woman to occupy the 'hot seat' in our ninety-odd-year history. I shall be able to retire knowing that, with Lesley, the business is in good hands and heart and that all our family, second, third, fourth and fifth generations, are right behind her – and Bettys.

Jonathan

Jonathan Wild
Director

CHAPTER 1

The History of Bettys

'So much tragedy all in one night...'

20th December, 1890

It hardly seems fair so close to Christmas: one small Swiss village, Wangen-an-der-Aare, suffering two unrelated family tragedies.

A mother of fourteen children threw herself into the icy waters of the River Aare and drowned; *'the result of a domestic altercation'*, the local paper said. A sad start – or end – to anyone's family history; but it wasn't mine.

That same night, by the same river, the paper reported, a fire broke out at the mill, the home of Johann Bützer, the miller and master-baker. Herr Bützer *'died because of his injuries and excessive inhalation of smoke causing inflammation of the lungs'*. His child, Maria Rosalia, also *'choked in the smoke during the fire, and was buried yesterday'*.

But the paper doesn't tell the whole story: only my family know it.

Amidst the smoke and the flames, Johann Bützer took his five-year-old son, Fritz, by one hand, and his seven-year-old daughter, Ida, by the other. To twelve-year-old Rosalia he shouted: *'Hang on to my night shirt tails!'* Meanwhile his second wife, Karolina, carried her two babes, one in each arm.

When they emerged safely from the mill, to the father's horror he realised that Rosalia had let go. She was still inside somewhere! Without hesitation he rushed back into the mill and died in vain trying to rescue her.

Two more deaths. *'So much tragedy all in one night'*, the newspaper concluded mournfully with typical Swiss understatement.

This story has been passed down through the family by the surviving daughter, Ida, my grandmother. Her little brother, Fritz, was destined not just to follow in his father's footsteps into the baking trade, but to create one of the most famous tea shops in the world.

For now, though, there was little hope for them. Their natural mother had died of TB three years earlier, so they were orphans.

Ida was taken to live with her stepmother's family. There was no room for Fritz so, as was the custom for orphans with no living relatives or family willing to take them in, he was sent back to the village of his ancestors, Teuffenthal, up in the mountains. There, as was the custom, he was literally auctioned off and 'bought' by a local farmer, who undertook to foster him: feed and clothe him and send him to school. However, the farmer gained not so much a foster child as free slave labour for his farm, for even a five-year-old can work, and won't complain too much if he is half starved and cruelly treated.

There Fritz stayed until he was free to leave on his fourteenth birthday. He was reunited with his sister Ida, completed his schooling, and became a trainee baker.

By 1903 Fritz was qualified. In his exams he scored particularly highly for his dough work but was otherwise signed off as merely capable. He was obviously destined for an unremarkable life in a small baker's shop in the Emmental valley. Even the excitement of compulsory military service passed him by. Fit and strong though he was from years of mixing bread dough with the power of his arms and shoulders alone, he failed his army medical because of his poor eyesight.

This is the farm-house in Tenftental where FB was forker-boy. Its still the original building as it might have looked to him on his way home from school.

Sketch by
Victor Wild

His imagination and ambition certainly weren't poor. After a childhood of serfdom he was determined now to make something of his life, to be a 'someone', to be his own master. He had intelligence, humour, great charm, and an appreciation of aesthetics and all things beautiful – especially girls! He was naturally inquisitive about the world and hungry to learn.

He wanted to master the arts not just of baking, but of confectionery and chocolate, too. He worked his way around Switzerland for three years before moving to Marseilles and then Paris. His sister Ida grew dizzy from so many postcards from so many distant cities!

Paris! What more could an ambitious Swiss village orphan ask for than to be a confectioner in Paris?

No, it still wasn't enough...

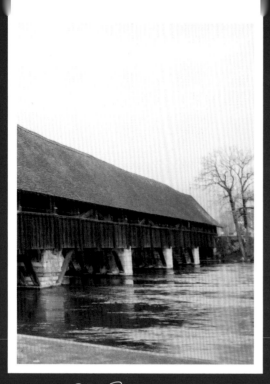

The River Aare

The historic covered bridge
by the mill at Wangen

The mill at Wangen-an-der-Aa

The façade survived the fire
and still stands today

Johann Bützer

Miller and master baker 1839–1890

Fritz Bützer

Happier days before the fire

Albert Ramstein FRIBOURG.

The young confectioner
Fritz, aged 19

Ida Bützer
Fritz's beloved sister

'From distant cities'
Fritz keeps his sister
up to date with his travels

'Maybe I will stay a while...'

12th September, 1907

A letter from Fritz Bützer to his sister Ida, translated from the original German, tells the story of his arrival in Yorkshire.

Meine Liebe Schwester,

Your long-expected letter arrived at last. I am much relieved to hear that all is well with you... As for me, you don't need to worry. I've travelled right across France and now across most of England too, with more good luck than calculation! Now I am in Bradford, a town of 450,000 in the north.

The journey was interesting, not to say 'bizarre et amusante...' I left Paris at 8.30 in the evening, after a jolly evening with cousin Adolphe who also gave me a bottle of wine for the journey. On the train I met a young Swiss businessman with his English sweetheart. We embarked at Dieppe, and at one in the morning we steamed off into total darkness and fog. The sea was heaving up and down, but the three of us promenaded on deck, or rather we fell about. But we were in great spirits, and we two Swiss started to sing some traditional songs. This went on until around 3.30am when my Swiss friend went to the railings to 'talk to the fishes'. We made fun of him, but after a while we joined him at the railing. He was so ill he collapsed on to the deck like a dishcloth. When the ticket collector came, I had to go through his pockets to find the documents.

By the time we reached England at 6am I could hardly stand either, and we three had the greatest difficulty in walking down the gangway, clutching each other desperately. In the train we fell fast asleep, and had to be rudely woken up by the conductor when we reached London.

My friends said goodbye, and I was left standing at the platform, suddenly realising that I had no idea where to find my train and what I had to do with all my luggage. What's more I had lost the address where I was meant to be going. There was a job – with whom? – waiting for me in a town – what town? All I could remember was that the name was something like 'Bratwurst'!

So there I was, not knowing a word of English, not even yes and no. I accosted everyone who came within reach, first in French and then in German, but all I got was blank looks. None of these idiots could speak anything but English!! Finally, a little old man offered to help with the few words of French he knew. If I wanted the train to Bratwurst I was not only on the wrong platform but in the wrong station. He escorted me to a cab, said something to the cabbie, and off I went I know not where.

A. B. 5004. DIEPPE. — Le Steamer « Dieppe »

The boat from Dieppe
Not always such a calm crossing!

The London train
On the right tracks, for the moment!

The train to 'Bratfort'
Illustration by Paul Slater, commissioned by *The Times*, March 2003

CHOCOLATE MAKERS

LUNCHEONS   TEAS

44 BONNET & SONS 44

BONNET & SONS   CONFECTIONERS.

Makers of the famous **Bonnet's Chocolate**.
At 2/6 Per lb.   By Post, 2/10.
LUNCHEON AND TEA ROOMS.
THE FASHIONABLE RENDEZVOUS OF BRADFORD.
44, DARLEY STREET, BRADFORD.

Bonnet's Chocolatiers

Fritz's first job in England, 1907

= **F. Belmont,** =
Chocolate Specialist.

Healthy and chic

Harrogate thrived as the premier
British health resort well into
the 1930s

Harrogate HEAL SALT
RHEUMATISM & LIVER SAL
FOR THE STOMAC
LIVER AND KIDNEY

HARROGATE
IT'S QUICKER BY RAIL
FREE GUIDE FROM F. J. C. BROOME, ROYAL BATHS, HARROGATE, OR ANY L·N·E·R OFFICE OR AGENCY

Harrogate H

They came to tak
would they prefer

'If I had failed, you would never have heard about it'

14th February, 1921

A letter from Fritz Bützer to his sister Ida, after an inexplicable silence of four years. Translated from the original German.

Meine Liebe Schwester,

At last I am able to write a few lines to you. First, my dear sister, please forgive me that I haven't written sooner. I have received your letters and the photographs of your children. My wife is quite jealous over them, especially the younger one. We have no children as yet. I am longing to see you again and I am glad that you are well and happy.

You will perhaps be curious to know what has happened to your 'dear' brother. Well, he is still the same dear old Fritz. He hasn't changed (my wife says the opposite) – anyway it's hardly surprising that one changes when the world spins round so fast.

'Fritz Bützer' anglicised into 'Frederick Belmont' by 1921

During the war I was working here in Harrogate and I became an English citizen and changed my name to Belmont. In my heart I am still the same old Bützer. As an Englishman I was duty bound to join the army and I was called up in November 1918. Luckily the armistice came and that was the end of my war fever. During this time I was able to save some money and in the spring of 1919 I founded a company. Now began a time of my life which I won't easily forget. You will understand what I mean when you read on.

'Muted pink panels' in Bettys Café

Menu illustration, 1930

Well, as I said, I formed a private company with a capital of £5,000 to found a first-class confiserie and café. My own share is one-quarter. A property was bought for £7,000. A mortgage was arranged and then came the equipping.

I must say here that I am the only shareholder who understands the business; the organising was totally on my shoulders. You can imagine what an effort it was to start such an exclusive business when the whole country was in a state of chaos after the world war.

Opening day was 17th July, 1919, and now came a time of 'either or', 'sink or swim'. Here I now had a shop exquisitely fitted out, the showcases in precious wood, mirrors and glass on the walls, the café furnished in grey, with muted pink panels with old-silver borders, with old-silver electric candleholders in the centres. On the second floor is a beautifully furnished Smoking Room. The china is grey-blue (white inside), the coffee and teapots in heavy nickel silver.

You can imagine what it all cost, and on top of that all the staff were new. Anyway, we opened, and the first day's takings were £30. After the first week I was sure of our success. Takings were £220. But I had my hands full. Not only did I have to supervise the production rooms on the third floor, but I also had to do the buying. At that time I had about twenty staff.

Quite soon the space turned out to be too small, and three months after the opening I looked around for more territory: the second building was opened on 1st August, 1920. Our turnover for 1920 was £17,000. You can imagine how I have my hands full. I am sending you some photos to show you how it looks.

The shop was 'exquisitely fitted out'

Menu illustration, 1930

Harrogate is a spa of the first order, and during the summer we had many well-known visitors as customers, for example, Lady Haig, Admiral Jellicoe, the Duke of Athlone, Princess Victoria (sister of King George V) etc.

Now my dear sister, you know what I have been doing and it's time I drew this long letter to a close. But I must say that I am very proud of my success. Yes, Ida, your brother has gambled and won, and you too shall have your share. Sometimes I wonder whether I wake or sleep. I couldn't bring myself to write to you during the critical time, and if I had failed you would never have heard about it. I only wish our mother was still alive.

I am sending you a photograph of us both taken at our wedding. And a photo of my wife. You can see she hasn't changed. Unfortunately she was very ill in March last year and had two operations. Now she is quite better. It was a difficult and expensive time for me. I am very happy. What I have I owe to my wife. She is not only my wife but my help and colleague.

Please remember me to all our relatives and friends. Your dear letters make me long for home and I shall come to Switzerland as soon as possible with my wife who longs to meet you.

Now I must close, my hand is heavy and I find it difficult to express myself fluently in my mother tongue.

Many greetings and kisses,

F Belmont

UNDER ROYAL PATRONAGE.

Betty's Ltd (HARROGATE)

THE EXCLUSIVE CAFÉ.

Opening day

The original Bettys Café, Harrogate, 1919

"LET'S GO TO BETTY'S

where we can meet our friends, and discuss things amongst surroundings that have the quiet harmony of perfect taste."

Good food, good cooking, and courteous personal service, are the features for which BETTY'S TEA ROOMS have become famous.

Morning Coffee, Luncheons, Afternoon Tea.

The latest gramophone and wireless set has been installed, and the World's Greatest Artistes can be heard in comfort, either on the wireless or gramophone.

Betty's Ltd The Exclusive Cafe.

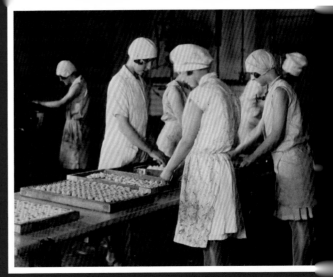

Another dream accomplished
Bettys Bakery opens, 1922

The new confectionery room

"LADY BETTY"
Peppermint
Creams

Bettys chocolate boxes
1920s

'Marvellous experience, but costly as usual...'

27th May, 1936

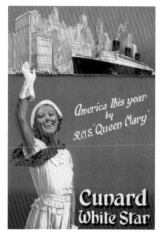

It was the society event of the year, if not the decade. On its maiden voyage from Southampton to New York, the great Cunarder, the *Queen Mary*, was packed with the great and the good. The first-class passenger list sparkled with stars from both sides of the Atlantic. The *Daily Sketch* recorded the sophisticated scene in the first-class dining saloon. Right in the centre of the photograph are Fritz Bützer and his wife, Claire. The Swiss foster child and his bride, now known to their friends as 'Dickie' and 'Bunny' Belmont, are mixing with the glitterati!

Dickie's new-fangled cine camera, bought especially for the trip, records glimpse after glimpse of the ankles, calves – and just a little more – of the leggy blonde starlets playing deck quoits.

A stroll around the promenade deck, a quarter of a mile, takes fifteen minutes, plus stoppage time to film a smile and a thigh or two. The Olympic runner, Lord Burghley, runs a lap of honour in full evening dress in less than sixty seconds, but these promenaders take it slow. They have to see and be seen, to film and be filmed.

It's a gruelling dining regime: breakfast at 8 or 9am; soup on deck at 11; lunch at 12.15 or 1.30; afternoon tea at 4; and dinner at 6.30 or 7.45.

A scene out in the Atlantic – in the magnificent first-class saloon of the Queen Mary.

Caught by the Daily Sketch, *29th May, 1936*

Frederick Belmont's original cine film footage from the maiden voyage of the Queen Mary

Looking at the *Daily Sketch* photograph, perhaps Dickie is suggesting an after-dinner visit to the card tables. He loves a flutter. Bunny reaches into her handbag for the ship's information booklet and sternly reminds Dickie that *'professional gamblers are reported as frequently travelling in Atlantic ships and passengers are warned to take precautions accordingly'.* So, he probably settles for a whisky and a cigar in a comfy sofa, and they reflect on their good fortune. 'This is the life, eh?'

The maiden voyage of the *Queen Mary* really was their extravagant trip of a lifetime. Dickie and Bunny wanted it to last forever. Of course they bought mementoes of the voyage for themselves, and little sailor dolls for the daughters of their friends; but they were cooking up an even more elaborate scheme to perpetuate the voyage. In his diary entry for 6th March, 1937, Dickie writes: *'Nearly another year since my last entry. Lots of things have happened since. First maiden voyage with* Queen Mary *to New York. Marvellous experience but very costly as usual. Further I acquired premises in York, excellent site, best in York for £25,750.'*

Now they would build their own *Queen Mary*! The liner's interior designers and shopfitters were hired. No expense was spared: walnut pillars and panelling, etched glass, exquisite marquetry... just like the great Cunarder: it was madness!

In 1999, eighty-three-year-old Harold Clark wrote to me of his *'many happy memories'* as an apprentice joiner working on Bettys York.

'I was loaned to Messrs Trollope & Colls, a London firm, whose tradesmen came down from Glasgow, where they had been fixing the panelling on the liner the Queen Mary, *and Bettys' panelling was to be the same.*

'Mr Belmont visited the premises every week and he was very kind always to leave a five pound note. My share was 10/- which was a lot of money when I was earning less than 20/- a week. When Mrs Belmont came she always kindly gave me a £1 note.

'I have had a wonderful working life with many memories, but none so dear as the time I worked at the new Bettys café in York and the great kindness of Mr & Mrs Belmont.'

CUNARD WHITE STAR

TO NEW YORK

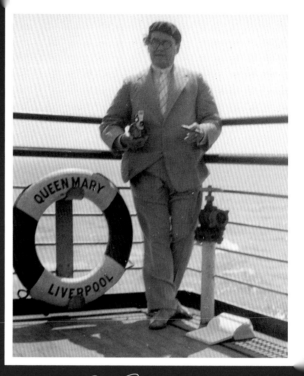

This is the life...
Dickie Belmont with his cine camera

At home on the ocean waves
Dickie and Bunny Belmont

The sailor doll
A souvenir from the voyage

Relaxing on the sun
First-class sunshine

Deck quoits
'Ankles, calves, and just a little bit more!'

Cunard White St

OBSERVATION LOUNGE & COCKTAIL BAR   R.M.S. "QUEEN MARY"   FIRST CLASS

GRILL   R.M.S. "QUEEN MARY"   VERANDAH

RESTAURANT   R.M.S. "QUEEN MARY"   FIRST CLASS

...And then there was Bettys York!

Bettys Ballroom

Dickie's diary, 16th June, 1937: *'We had a great opening at York on June 1st. Lord Middleton performed the opening. We had a good send off. At the same time I still regret that we took York. It will be a great worry and responsibility. I was wonderfully situated financially and I reprove myself daily for opening York. I do not anticipate great returns; well, it is done now and so I must carry on and make the best of it. Bunny has been a little brick. She helped me marvellously. She has any amount of pluck.'*

It has been eighteen years since they opened their first tea room in Harrogate. A purpose-built bakery followed in 1922; then a tea room in Bradford in 1924. This latter venture was a great delight to Dickie; for the premises he took over were none other than those of Bonnet's, his first employers in 1907. Leeds followed in 1930. His diary entry for 28th March, 1931 records: *'Well it is done. Leeds is proving a great success. We opened with a great noise and in good style. It is really gratifying to have accomplished my ambitions.'*

This was a rare note of optimism. The reality was that Bettys was not a gold mine. Dickie always, always wanted his cafés 'just so', and would invest lavishly even when the company didn't have the money.

Diary entry for 4th August, 1930: *'Anticipate Leeds expenses to be £6,500 in all. I have only £1,500 so far.'* 2nd October, 1930: *'Seen bank managers, things are a little critical financially. Well anything worth having is worth fighting for.'* 28th March, 1931: *'Leeds has proved much more costly; I think we have spent £8,500.'*

Things improved significantly for Bettys early in 1936 when Dickie sold the freeholds to the Harrogate and Leeds properties and leased them back. Even so, a few months after the *Queen Mary* voyage he recorded that *'the financial position is still rather tight but I think by persevering we will be able to manage.'*

Whatever will the boy ask for next, Mary!
In this morning's letter he writes:

" *Dear Mater,—Please send me a sponge, toothpaste, pair of tennis shoes, a feeding trough for my white mice, a pocket knife with J.R. on. and four pounds of BETTY'S Assorted Cream Fudge. Your loving John.*
P.S.—If Betty's Cream Fudge makes the parcel too heavy don't send the other things. XXX "

OF PARAMOUNT IMPORTANCE to the boy, because of the delicious moments of enjoyment whilst eating them. You would find the same enjoyment whilst trying them. Include a pound on your weekend shopping list.

Betty's Ltd

THE EXCLUSIVE CAFE,
CAMBRIDGE CRESCENT, HARROGATE.
MAKERS OF DELICIOUS SWEETMEATS IN A MODEL FACTORY.

1929

As for his personal finances, they were even worse! Whatever capital he did save he used to buy Bettys shares from the investors who had put up the original capital to start the business. The diary entries for the 1930s are peppered with assessments of his personal finances: *'Unsatisfactory. I wonder when it will improve'*; *'Actually entered a newspaper Derby competition with a view to make money. I could do with £200 to settle everything up. Don't know what to do'; 'still unsatisfactory', 'still bad', 'still very poor',* and a few months after the *Queen Mary* voyage: *'My affairs are still not too good but might and could be worse! I am thinking of flying to Switzerland to see my sister and the children. I do not yet know if I shall go or not. We went for a staff trip, 120 of them... well I am proud of them and of my firm.'*

Adverts commissioned from T. J. Bond, a well-known illustrator of the era

"We shall not be in for lunch Mary — we will lunch at Betty's"

An excellent lunch for discriminating people. Good food, well served.

Four Course Lunch 2/-
or A La Carte.

HARROGATE - LEEDS - BRADFORD.

1933

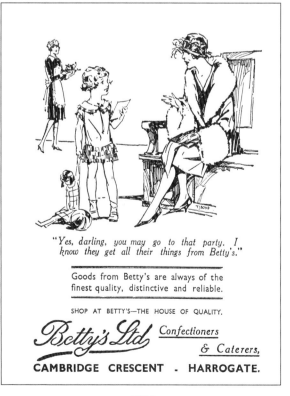

"Yes, darling, you may go to that party. I know they get all their things from Betty's."

Goods from Betty's are always of the finest quality, distinctive and reliable.

SHOP AT BETTY'S—THE HOUSE OF QUALITY.

Betty's Ltd Confectioners & Caterers,

CAMBRIDGE CRESCENT - HARROGATE.

1936

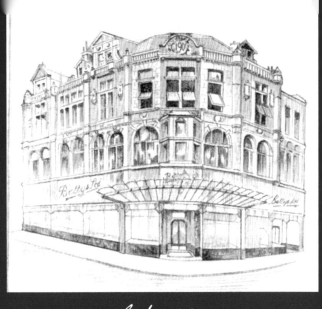

Bradford, 1924
The second Bettys included the 'Mayfair' function rooms

Leeds, 1930
The third Bettys at the corner of
Commercial Street and Lands Lane

STAFF OUTING WINDERMERE

*B*ETTY'S (*Harrogate*) *Ltd.,*
have pleasure in announcing
that their new restaurant in
St. Helen's Square, York,
will be open to the public on
Tuesday, *June* 1, at 11 a.m.

Lord Middleton has
graciously consented to
open the premises.

The honour of your
patronage is invited.

York, 1937

The official opening of the fourth Bettys, 1st June, 1937

BETTY'S STAFF TRIP.

MOTOR TOUR TO THE LAKE DISTRICT.

Five chars-a-bancs accommodating about 120 employees of Betty's Ltd. from Starbeck, Leeds, Bradford, and Harrogate, started at 7-30 a.m. on Sunday for a motor tour to the Lake District. Breakfast was served in the country about two hours later, and after a short stay at Ambleside a stop was made at Keswick for lunch. At 4-30 the return journey was begun.

The trip was favoured with exceptionally fine weather. After an early mist and some rain the sky became almost cloudless. The route lay through beautiful country, and the drive was greatly appreciated.

At 8-30 supper was served at Hellifield. Replying to a vote of thanks from the staff, Mr. F. Belmont (chairman and managing director) said the directors appreciated the close co-operation and harmony that existed between the management and the staff, and that each employee was individually responsible for the success of the firm, and it was gratifying to know that in spite of difficult times the number of employees had reached 142.

After a hearty sing-song a sunburnt happy crowd made for home.

Harrogate Advertiser, 1931

'It is like a fairy story'

2nd October, 1952

It was a sunny Saturday morning. He may have been sixty-seven years old but Dickie Belmont still enjoyed the company of a lady, especially a Swiss one! Whilst the public thronged the cafés on the ground and first floors of his Harrogate premises, in his second-floor office Dickie was having a very private cup of coffee with his great friend Wanda. A Swiss émigré like himself, Wanda too was now anglicised, and they spoke together in English. No one overheard their conversation, so we have to imagine him reflecting on his good fortune and many mishaps over the last fifteen years. 'This is the life!' he would have said, but there would have been sadness in his voice. Everything had not gone his way.

True, business had prospered, especially at York. A full publican licence had been obtained for York *'for the paltry sum of £1,000 from Sir William Foster Todd'*, his diary records. *'What a stroke of luck. It is like a fairy story. Our balance sheet shows profit for York £5,000 and £14,000 for the company.'*

Then there was war. Food shortages and staff shortages brought the business to its knees, in spite of the insatiable demand from the public. The Canadian bomber pilots who were based at a dozen or more airfields around York made Bettys Bar in York their home. Five hundred of them scratched their names on a mirror behind the bar with a diamond ring. Many of these airmen died, many were decorated, many returned years later with their families to show them their signatures.

The basement bar at Bettys (now the Oakroom) was known as 'The Dive'. The reputation of the Canadian airmen for charm, good looks and deep pockets spread around Yorkshire, and at weekends charabancs of girls from Leeds would descend on the 'Dive' along with the local talent. It was a bittersweet party time.

Busy though Bettys York was in wartime, the authorities twice proposed to requisition it for official use. Dickie Belmont smiled at the memory of his ripostes, both times so short and sharp that the authorities relented, realising that to close Bettys was unthinkable.

An incendiary bomb crashing through the roof nearly did close Bettys York, though. Tom the van man was the duty firewatcher that night, and bravely put the fire out before it could take hold.

Around the rest of the Bettys branches, Dickie recalled, the challenge was to concoct meals out of powdered egg, fish scraps, grey 'utility' flour and the more exotic supplies sent over from America: corned beef, tinned spaghetti and beans. Restaurants were not permitted to charge more than five shillings for a three-course meal.

Bettys were better than most at eking out their supplies and always had the largest queues in town. Once, Dickie bought a lorry-load of burnt and sooty honey salvaged from a burnt-out London warehouse. He turned it into fudge, a delicacy – like all sweet things – so rare that people queued down the street for a small piece.

Catering for wartime weddings was a nightmare. On more than one occasion the bride had to make do with a fully iced cardboard box instead of a cake. Whatever the improvisation, the brides were invariably grateful.

By the end of the war Dickie's morale was so low and the company's finances so poor that he actually sold Bettys York to North British Hotels. In fact he felt like selling out altogether. It wasn't as if he had a family to share his business with. Only pride in his beloved creation kept him going.

'We have no children yet,' Dickie had written to his sister in 1921. Dickie and Bunny never did have any children. At the age of 51 Dickie, anxious for an heir to take on his business, asked his sister Ida in Switzerland if he could have one of her three teenagers to bring up as his own.

Ida was struggling to make ends meet as her husband, Carl Conrad Wild, spent most of his income from his accounting job at St Gallen town hall publishing his philosophical writings at his own expense and hiring halls to give public speeches on world peace. He was horrified at mankind's inability to create a better world, and was determined to make a difference personally.

Dickie and Bunny visit Ida in Switzerland, 1930

At one stage he gave up his clerical job to set up a business bringing sweetness and light to his fellow countrymen. Reading how ancient civilisations believed in the special powers of honey, he decided he would reinvigorate the Swiss people by selling them honey by the spoonful, daily, door-to-door. The young sales girls who he employed were instructed to seal each sticky transaction with a kiss. The venture was not a success. No wonder his family were impoverished.

Carl Conrad Wild

5TH PARA BATT
REG COULTAS
5TH PARA BRIGADE
KEN. RUDDY
6 OCT 1943

61 SQ 77
RCAF W. Quigley

The Dive

Bettys' infamous bar and a selection of signatures from the wartime mirror

"WING DING"
Sgt. Brullinger

J N Fletcher
R.C.A.F.
VANCOUVER, BC
CANADA

J E McDonald
420 RCAF
1-2-45

S L McCulloch
R C57311 RCAF
H24 spodn

The requisition letters

1 Queens Road,
HARROGATE.

REF.NO:5AC/21.

11th August, 1943.

The Secretary,
Messrs Betty's Ltd.,
8/11 Cambridge Crescent,
Harrogate.

SUBJECT: BETTY'S CAFE, DAVYGATE, YORK.

Dear Sirs,

with reference to your premises in Davygate, York, I should be glad if you would let me know what your reactions would be if the whole of your premises mentioned above were requisitioned.

Would you please also inform me what you would expect in the way of compensation rental.

Yours faithfully,

J Manson Capt

Lieut-Colonel,
No. 5 Area.

12th August, 1943

Dear Sir,

We acknowledge receipt of your letter dated 11th August with very great concern. We must point out that we serve an average of 20,000 (twenty thousand) Main meals, Subsidiary meals, Teas and Hot beverages, per week. In addition we are retailers of bread and flour confectionery. The Bars are also popular and are largely patronised by the forces.

We maintain that we perform an essential public service in York and we sincerely hope that you will not find it necessary to commandeer the establishment.

We trust to be favoured with an interview at your convenience.

Yours faithfully,
BETTY'S (HARROGATE) LTD.,

Chairman and Managing Director.

Lieut. Colonel,
Quartering Command No. 5 Area,
1, Queen's Road,
Harrogate.

"Here's Betty's Bar"

A popular wartime haunt

Bettys Bar was so famous that it even featured in a cartoon in the *Tatler*

...and only thirty minutes 'til closing time.

Canadian airmen would do anything to get to Bettys Bar

A FULL-SCALE A.R.P. TEST, the first of its kind, took place in Harrogate on Sunday.

The Bettys ambulance

Once the bread was delivered, Bettys vans help with the war effort, 1940

REF:NO:5QC/21.
JGH/CFGT.

1 Queens Road,
HARROGATE

SUBJECT: BETTY'S CAFE, DAVYGATE, YORK.

13th August, 1943.

The Secretary,
Messrs Betty's Ltd.,
Cambridge Crescent,
Harrogate.

Dear Sirs,

I acknowledge receipt of your letter of the 12th instant, and in view of the contents it is not proposed to continue with the requisitioning of the above named property.

Yours faithfully,

Lieut-Colonel,
Quartering Commandant, No. 5 Area.

War is over — Smile please!

The ladies of Bettys Harrogate

In March 1936 Ida's thirteen-year-old son, Carl Viktor Wild, volunteered for the English adventure. Like his uncle before him, he arrived speaking not a word of English. He was groomed first as an English gentleman at Sedbergh, the Yorkshire Dales boarding school. In the holidays he worked in the bakery and used his artistic talent to design advertisements for Bettys. Then began his catering training. Never mind the blitz and the doodlebugs, Dickie sent Victor to the best hotel in London, Claridge's, to train.

Victor Wild's reconstruction of his original 1943 artwork

While the exiled crowned heads of Europe swanned around in the elegant public rooms and suites of Claridge's, Victor spent month after month in the underground kitchens cleaning chickens and gutting fish. To this day he has no idea what the hotel looks like. To keep himself sane, Victor rented an attic room nearby, hired a piano, and passed the time between shifts playing music, drawing, and painting. News of his artistic ability spread to the kitchens at Claridge's, a hotbed of communists, and he was asked to design posters for a new hotel workers' union. War or no war, Victor recalls, conditions were abominable.

As soon as the war was over Victor returned to Switzerland, training in hotels and restaurants in Zürich, Pontresina, and his home town of St Gallen.

Dickie Belmont wasn't sure whether Victor would ever come back. Victor had missed his mother sorely – and his sisters – and wasn't overly anxious to come back to a country still beset with shortages and rationing. However, return he did, in 1948, and the much-relieved Dickie became more positive about the future. Victor persuaded him to try and buy Bettys York back, which he did in 1950 for less than he had sold it for in 1947! It was to York, to the biggest Bettys of them all, that Victor was sent as trainee manager.

By 1952 Dickie had more family around him than just Victor. On holiday on the south coast in the summer of 1946, Dickie and Bunny were captivated by a bonny baby on the beach. They determined to adopt her and give her the chance of a better life. So arrived Valerie, a delightful two-year-old.

Fifty-five-year-old Bunny sought out a nurse to help her with this new parenting challenge. So arrived Kay. As is usual in our family, hearts fluttered. Soon Victor married Kay and started a family of his own.

On that sunny Saturday morning of 2nd October, 1952 Kay was pushing their big carriage pram down Otley Road in Harrogate with two-year-old Elizabeth and four-month-old Jonathan on board.

Valerie Belmont, a daughter for Bunny and Dickie

Victor Wild

Learning to be
an English gentleman, 1936

Victor and his fellow chefs

St Gallen, 1945

We have pleasure in announcing

that

BETTY'S CAFE RESTAURANT St. Helen's Sq., York

IS NOW AGAIN UNDER THE FULL CONTROL OF
THE ORIGINAL OWNERS *Betty's Cafes* LTD.

HARROGATE

YOU WILL FIND THERE THE SAME HIGH QUALITY FOOD
AND COURTEOUS SERVICE AS IN OUR OTHER ESTABLISHMENTS
AT HARROGATE, LEEDS AND BRADFORD

*WE INVITE YOUR PATRONAGE
ON YOUR NEXT VISIT TO YORK*

PUTTING IT PAT.

Amazing But True!

38,814 lbs. of Butter have been used by Betty's
during the past 12 months in their various productions.

Our schoolboy artist estimates that if made into
butter pats and placed on top of each other they
would make a column

8¾ MILES HIGH.

ALL Betty's products are made of best butter.
Another reason why the quality of our products is
always reliable and uniform.

Betty's Ltd
(HARROGATE)

**HARROGATE
LEEDS
BRADFORD
YORK**

Jonathan and Elizabeth Wild

Posing for the press, Easter 1953

Kay Wild

New Year's Eve, 1950

Advertisement designed
by schoolboy artist Victor Wild, 1939

Victor Wild's cartoon of himself, 1948

Whilst Dickie and Wanda were reminiscing over coffee in Harrogate, in York that same October morning Victor was in the kitchens ensuring everything was ready for a busy lunchtime. He was called to the phone; it was Miss Leggett from the Harrogate office. She told him that Mr Belmont had collapsed in his office. The doctor had been called and was with him, but she feared he had passed away.

Victor drove straight to Harrogate and found his uncle's body laid out on the office floor. There was no way that his body could be carried respectfully down the winding back stairs of the building. He would have to be carried down the front stairs, past the café, and out through the shop. Closing Bettys for the day was unthinkable, so Victor kept a vigil over the body until 5.30pm, when the undertakers arrived to carry Frederick 'Dickie' Belmont away from Bettys, privately and with dignity.

Twenty years earlier Dickie Belmont had written in his diary:

'I shall point out some remarks about what are the best things in life.
I think the following;

1) Enough money to be independent.

2) The glow you get from giving somebody something, which is far more glowing than the glow you get from receiving something (except a thick ear).

3) Sleep. Really I think this ought to be higher.

4) Landing at any seaport after a rough journey.'

Dickie was an intermittent diarist. Had he ever revised the entry he might have scribbled underneath:

'5) And the best way to end life is to be taken by surprise, surrounded by what one loves best.'

Victor Wild's cartoon of Dickie Belmont, 1948

A sixtieth birthday card drawn by Victor for his uncle

In the fairy stories the frog prince lives happily ever after. Fritz Bützer, the poor Swiss orphan transformed into Frederick 'Dickie' Belmont, English entrepreneur, probably died happily ever after, sitting in Bettys, with the premises full to bursting with customers anxious to have a taste of what he had created, and willing to pay good money for it: What a way to go, eh? What a way to go...

The *Harrogate Herald,* November, 1947

'Best Boss'

'He's the best boss in the world. He's more than a boss, he's a friend,' said Mary. And everyone round her agreed. She was standing, wine glass in hand, on the beautifully carpeted floor, which, twenty-eight years ago, she had scrubbed the night before the 'boss', had opened his business for the first time. Mr F. W. Belmont, founder and proprietor of a Harrogate café, is the 'boss' and Mary, with other departmental heads of the firm, had invited him to his own café on Wednesday evening so that they could present him and Mrs Belmont with his portrait. Mr Belmont, a Swiss, arrived in England forty years ago and made his way to Bradford, arriving completely penniless. He took a job in a confectionery business and quickly decided that he would start his own firm.

The portrait presented to Mr Belmont on Wednesday was painted by Mr John A. Berrie, the eminent artist who recently painted Lord Mountbatten's portrait. Mr Berrie was present on Wednesday's unveiling and received many congratulations from the staff on his execution of their commission.

HE IS TRYING TO MAKE US BELIEVE THAT HE IS ONLY TASTING THE WINES TO SEE IF THEY ARE FIT TO SELL.

But there is one thing about our boss — he is always ready to help —

Early day
Staff outing
Whitby, 1921

At home
His last trip t
Switzerland

'In the right direction, I hope'

20th July, 1962

A new diary to peep into: my father Victor Wild's. *'C. E. Taylor agreement signed at £180,000. A big step for Bettys! In the right direction, I hope.'*

It had all started with an overheard conversation in Bettys in Harrogate. Naturally, Bettys customers can chatter away about gossip and scandal knowing that Bettys waitresses will hear everything but listen to nothing. They are the soul of discretion. Well, usually; there are exceptions.

In the spring of 1962, the café manager, Miss May Carter, who had served Bettys for over thirty years, excitedly told my father that she had overheard some businessmen talking about the Taylor family putting their business up for sale. Like Bettys, C. E. Taylor & Co. was a Yorkshire tea shop business, but whilst Bettys had a bakery at its heart and soul, Taylors had a little tea and coffee importing, blending, and roasting business.

Victor leapt into action and made an immediate offer at the asking price of £180,000, having secured a large bank loan. Why on earth did he take such a huge risk?

Dickie Belmont's sudden demise in October 1952 nearly led to the death of Bettys. Heavy death duties were payable, and the company almost had to be sold. Victor Wild was thrust into the role of managing director and at twenty-nine years old he felt totally unprepared for the task ahead. Bunny Belmont was the new chairman, but she was already tired and retired.

It took ten hard years for Victor to stabilise Bettys; to deal with the tax issues and rebuild the product range and menu after years of rationing. Victor always says that it was Kay's steady help and support that made all the difference.

As Victor gained in confidence, he wanted to prove himself not just as a steward of his uncle's creation, but as an entrepreneur in his own right. He opened a late-night espresso bar in Street Lane in Leeds, but the 'bike boys' – mods and rockers – proved too hard to handle. He opened a smart Italian restaurant in the basement of Bettys York. He bought a house to accommodate all the Italian chefs and waiters, but their romantic antics proved too hot to handle. He opened a continental delicatessen next to Bettys in Harrogate, which introduced northerners to a whole new world of delicacies that we now take for granted. All these were ahead of their time, anticipating the less conservative, more experimental mood of the 1960s.

![Bettys logo]

Miss May Carter
and the Italian waiters

Is she telling them about the sale of Taylors?

Victor Wild

Takes the helm at
age twenty-nine

The Coffee Shop
Street Lane, Leeds

Bettys
Delicatessen

A novelty for
the North

The Oakroom Restaurant

The Italian waiters at Bettys York

Now, in 1962, the purchase of Taylors was Victor's opportunity to prove himself his uncle's worthy successor.

The founder of Taylors, Charles Edward Taylor, was born on 31st July, 1866. His Quaker father, once a pea-dealer, was now a master-grocer in York.

All the Taylor children went to Quaker schools, and it was Quaker connections that landed the two eldest Taylor boys apprenticeships in London with the Ashby family's tea and coffee business. Whilst Llewellyn, the eldest son, was a great success following his training as a tea and coffee taster, Charles Edward struggled. Llewellyn became a sales manager and was later offered a directorship at Ashbys. Young Charles – and he was still a teenager at the time – was sent to pioneer sales in the south-west. He felt that in this part of the country both the water and the clientele were very different, so he continually asked the Ashbys' buyers to source him teas specially suited for this market. Teas were stockpiled, but young Charles was unable to sell them. He was sacked.

They say failure is not in falling down, but in staying down. Encouraged by his father and elder brother, Charles decided to set up his own tea and coffee business in Yorkshire. Llewellyn became his sleeping partner, providing financial backing and, through Ashbys, buying his tea and coffee at the weekly London auctions.

Charles opened a small warehouse in Park Row in Leeds, but quickly realised that there was too much well-established competition. Instead, he looked to the booming new spa towns of Harrogate and Ilkley, where he opened 'Kiosk' tea and coffee shops with tasting rooms attached where local guest-house proprietors could come and taste his wares and choose blends precisely right for their local water source.

It wasn't long before the tasting rooms became cafés, dark and smoky like the old London coffee houses, where local businessmen met, with runners bringing documents from their offices so they could spend the whole day drinking coffee.

In 1896 Charles ventured further into catering, opening a much more genteel café in Ilkley, the Café Imperial, and in 1905 another Café Imperial in Harrogate in a newly built mock Scottish baronial castle at the top of Parliament Street.

Further Kiosks were opened in Wakefield and Keighley and St Anne's-on-Sea, and Taylors also took over the catering at The Tea House in Harrogate's Valley Gardens, at the Winter Gardens, and at the Royal Spa Concert Rooms. Charles and Llewellyn each had one son, who they groomed for succession, starting like themselves with training with Ashbys in London. The Great War intervened. Llewellyn's son, Bernard, served in the cavalry. He returned safe and sound, but the ghastly experience of the Western Front made him want to live each day to the full, to have a good time rather than take business too seriously. Charles's son, Douglas, lied about his age and joined up at seventeen. He returned within a few weeks with a badly injured hip. Always a timid, languorous lad, Douglas became neurotically insecure. Only strict routines and the minimum of stress kept him sane.

Both cousins served as directors, but, having no children themselves, looked to their wider family for someone to run the business for them. Just as Frederick Belmont found a nephew, my father, to 'adopt' as his successor, so too did the Taylors find a nephew to provide succession.

Bernard's wife, a music-hall star whom he had courted and won at the stage door, had an equally theatrical sister, a Shakespearean actress who was always on tour. As she needed a permanent home for her young son James Raleigh, the Taylors 'adopted' him. When he left school in 1920, he was sent to London to learn the tea and coffee trade at Ashbys before joining the family business. James served the Taylor family loyally and became chairman in 1956.

James had no children either, so with no succession and a declining business with little profit, the family decided to put the ailing business up for sale, and realise the value of their properties if nothing else.

The Sign of Good Service.

James stayed on after the takeover by Bettys in 1962, 'just for a few months' to help with the transition and look after the highly specialist job of tea and coffee buyer. In the end, he stayed on another twenty-five years and trained both my brother and me, as well as our present head coffee buyer.

Bettys now owned nine cafés in all, including three in Harrogate. It took more than a decade for Victor and Kay to sort these properties out. Victor decided not to drop the Taylors family name, and all its history with it, but to focus it on its roots, in tea and coffee importing. Bettys would stay as the name for his tea shops and bakery, and the best of the buildings were converted to Bettys. The present Bettys Harrogate is the old Taylors Café Imperial; similarly the present Bettys Ilkley is the former Taylors Kiosk café. Little Bettys in York was also formerly a Kiosk café.

At the end of his diary entry for 20th July, 1962, Victor writes:
'On October 2nd it will be 10 years since Uncle died. Auntie tells me he once nearly accepted a job with C. E. Taylors in 1918.'

This reversal of fortunes is an irony which Dickie Belmont would have loved.

The Kiosk Cafe and Tea and Coffee Stores,

Charles Taylor
1866–1942

The first Taylors Kiosk
16 Parliament Street, Harrogate

Llewellyn Taylor
1861–1935

Taylors in the Valley Gardens
Municipal catering at its finest
at the beginning of the twentieth century

Fashionable Ilkley, 1900
The Kiosk Ilkley is now Bettys

The Café Imperial, 1924
Taylors occupied the site of the present-day Bettys in Harrogate

A gift from his staff
Charles Taylor's pocket watch

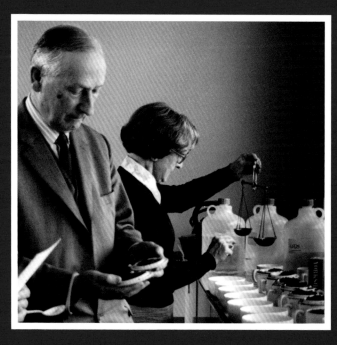

Taylors Tea
Taylors' 'Pagoda Tea Tips'
was the forerunner of
Yorkshire Tea

James Raleigh, 1907—1999
Taylors' last chairman and tea taster extraordinaire

A Diamond Jubilee

17th July, 1979

Bettys celebrated its sixtieth anniversary in style. Having joined the family business four years earlier, I was put in charge of the celebrations.

There was music in the cafés, just as there had been in the days when Miss Maude Niner and Madame Cholmondeley-Harrop had held sway.

Customers who could find any pre-metric coinage could pay for their tea or coffee at 1919 prices.

We revived a whole collection of Frederick Belmont's fancies, which we hadn't made for years: 'Sarah Bernhardts', 'Chocolate Leopolds', and 'Mr Belmont's Kirsch Cigar' – best truffle, of course!

There was a Diamond Jubilee Ball for 600 staff and their partners and a special Diamond Jubilee bonus equivalent to three months' pay for every member of staff.

Betty's Ltd

The exclusive
CAFE
Under Royal and distinguished patronage.

SPECIAL NOTICE
We have engaged for the Winter Season
MISS MAUDE NINER,
Solo Violiniste from the Queens Hall and Albert Hall, London.

Accompaniste:
Mdme. CHOLMONDELEY-HARROP.

1921

I don't think we realised it at the time but Bettys' Diamond Jubilee was the wake-up call for the third generation, and it shaped the way the business was to be run for the next thirty years. My wife, Lesley, joined the business then, followed by – for a few years at least – my brother Tony and my sister Elizabeth.

At the heart of our thinking was the desire to get right back in touch with the 'original sparks' that had ignited the ambitions of Frederick Belmont and Charles Taylor. Both were craftsmen, driven perfectionists with an eye for detail. Yet both were visionaries, progressive – almost radical – in their thinking. Both would have been flattered to have their values treated with such respect by future generations; both would have been even more pleased to see their Swiss and Yorkshire heritage shaped and made contemporary by each generation.

Diamond Jubilee celebrations
Paraphernalia from July 1979

My...J.Wild......
is cordially invited to

Bettys

DIAMOND JUBILEE BALL
at Middlethorpe Hall York
THURSDAY 26 JULY 1979 8 PM - 1AM

Staff H/W Guest

Please Bring This Ticket With You

No 536

Bettys

DIAMOND JUBILEE BALL
at
Middlethorpe Hall York
THURSDAY 26 JULY 1979   8 PM - 1 AM

IN THE GARDEN
Barbeque & Buffet · Brass Band · Fairground Stalls · Steel Band

IN THE HALL
Dancing with two Discos and Steel Band · Three Bars · Pool Competition · Wine Bar

TICKETS

Staff -
Staff Tickets Free

Guests -
(only one per member of staff)
Husband/Wife Free
Other Guest £3·50

...ase sign ticket application list by   JULY 7

Kay and Victor Wild
At the Jubilee Ball

CHOCOLATE LEOPOLD
rum & marzipan fancies

SARAH BERNHARDT
buttercream & fondant fancies

Curd Tarts
1½ᴰ each

Mr Belmont's fancies
Taken from his original recipe book

In the last thirty years, my generation has sought to resist the temptation to treat 'Bettys' and 'Taylors' as concepts or brands, but rather revere them as something more authentic. That's what we have tried to achieve, anyway; and I say 'we' because Bettys and Taylors in these decades has not just been about Lesley and me. My parents did not retire from the board until 1996, and, as well as my brother and sister, my cousin Valerie and her son Richard have all worked in the business and contributed enormously to its success.

It has not always been easy working together as a family. We are all rather sensitive, creative souls, but with that inherited single-minded competitive streak that sometimes leads to fall-outs. They say tension can be creative, but I prefer the harmony that prevails most of the time.

Nowadays the business is too diverse for one person, or even one family, to be experts at everything. Lesley and I have brought together and trained teams of some of the best craftsmen in the world: tea tasters, coffee masters, chocolatiers, bakers, confectioners, and cooks, and not forgetting the waiting staff who soothe your jangled nerves. Each generation of our craftsmen has to be more skilled than their predecessors: we couldn't survive otherwise.

We are still in the middle of the 'third-generation years'. I am too close to it and *so* I don't want to write too much about it. It is still a colourful, living story and not ready to be captured as sepia-tinted history *just yet*.

I will say that two things have characterised the years since Bettys' Diamond Jubilee in 1979.

Innovative as usual, 1927

COME TO A YORKSHIRE TEA TO-DAY

A NEW INNOVATION.

Betty's Ltd., beg to announce that they have introduced in their Cafe a little surprise for their many patrons in the form of a

YORKSHIRE TEA 1/3
AT AN INCLUSIVE COST OF

Consisting of :—Tea or Coffee, with Cream; One Sandwich—Egg and Cress, York Ham or Potted Beef Steak; Special Yorkshire Teacake—toasted— or Hot Buttered Scone; One Cake— Plain, Fancy, or Cream.

This Tea is daintily served in the luxurious surroundings, which is exclusively " Betty's."

THE ORCHESTRA PLAYS FROM 3-30 to 5-33 DAILY.

Betty's Ltd

CAMBRIDGE CRESCENT HARROGATE,

THE EXCLUSIVE CAFE

AND AT 42 & 44, DARLEY STREET, BRADFORD.

Tea to suit the water: old-fashioned quality exported to twenty-five countries

First has been learning to live with the success we have had taking Bettys' expertise and products to a wider audience. We have never wanted to spoil the spirit of Bettys by turning her into a chain. Instead we have made specialist products like Yorkshire Tea, and sold them around the world. We never realised what an appetite there would be for old-fashioned quality.

Secondly, we have had to learn how to keep a family atmosphere in a business which now has well over 1,000 staff. We have a wonderful leadership team, of which Lesley and I are only a small part. By staying solely Yorkshire-based, we endeavour to preserve a family feel, but it is still our greatest challenge.

The Diamond Jubilee taught us to celebrate in style. Our staff balls have always been grand affairs, but a more practical celebration of success is the regular profit-sharing bonus paid to all our staff, even to newcomers and students. These are examples of the family's commitment to its extended family of staff: to their training, their welfare, their pride, and their pleasure.

Bettys generally appears calm, almost becalmed in its traditions. Not much for us to do, you might say, other than manage the queues. The reality is that we have to run very fast to appear to be standing still. One look at the changes to our menus over the years shows how hard we have to work to make our traditions contemporary in each generation. Tradition is a living thing, after all.

It is nearly sixty years since my great-uncle Frederick Belmont died. I never knew him; I have no memories of him. He died when I was four months old.

I am sitting in his old office chair now. In front of me is his little smoking cabinet in which he kept his cigars. When I was born he gave my mother a gift to be kept and presented to me on my twenty-first birthday. It was a Jamaica Savana cigar. I smoked it at my birthday party.

The stewardship of his business was another gift, one which I have had to grow into over thirty-five years. It has been a real struggle for me and I forget how many times I have handed in my notice to my father! Thank goodness I have now handed over to Lesley!

If my great-uncle could come back down to earth just for one day, what would I want to show him of the present-day Bettys? Not just the buildings and traditions of his that we have preserved; those would flatter him but not stir him. No, what would excite – and I hope delight – him would be our newest ventures. But let's visit it all. Why not follow behind us...

Bettys has always moved with the times, 1929

CHAPTER 2

The Present Day

A Grand Day Out

Every Bettys is full of temptations. We have built our business on lifting people's spirits with simple pleasures.

The countryside between the Bettys branches is full of temptations too.

Whether you travel by car, bicycle or Harley-Davidson (yes, we have regulars who do!), or on foot, if you leave the highways for the byways you are in for a treat.

In the boot of my car, for the last twenty years, I have carried a rucksack full of walking clothes. I have had this dream that one sunny day, on my way to work at Ilkley or Northallerton, I will run away to the hills. Alas, duty is a powerful presence in a family business, and I have never used my 'running away rucksack'...yet! Now, with retirement on the horizon I may get the chance to explore the 'temptations' in-between the Bettys, and even write about them.

It always surprises me how many people visit two or even three different Bettys branches on the same day. It is perfectly possible to visit all six in a day – even on a bicycle. The annual 'Fat Rascal Charity Ride', organised by keen Bettys cyclists along with the York Peddlers, takes in refreshment stops at all the Bettys branches along its 120-mile circular route. It is a grand day out!

The map here is a reminder of how wonderfully situated all the Bettys Café Tea Rooms are. Never far from the Yorkshire Dales and the North York Moors National Parks, Bettys have the best landscapes in the country on their doorstep. Yet the conurbations of Leeds, Bradford, even Manchester and east Lancashire, are not too far way. No wonder my great-uncle decided to 'stay a while'.

We constantly receive letters suggesting we open a Bettys in such-and-such a town or city, in the UK and overseas. My reply has always been for such a self-sufficient business as ours it is not practical for daily deliveries to be more than thirty miles from our bakery. And the special family intimacy of Bettys requires us all to be in close contact: to spread ourselves too widely would risk spoiling that.

There is another reason too. One of the few pieces of my father's advice I have listened to is: *'Don't open a business anywhere you are not prepared to travel once a week, and enjoy the journey.'*

SWALEDALE

WENSLEYDALE

YORKSHIRE
DALES
NATIONAL PARK

NIDDERDALE

WHARFEDALE

A59

Bettys

NORTHALLERTON

NORTH
YORK
MOORS
NATIONAL PARK

A19

HOWARDIAN HILLS

Bettys
HARLOW
CARR.

Otley

Bettys
HARROGATE

A59

LITTLE BETTYS CAFE

Bettys
YORK

ILKLEY

BETTYS CAFE TEAR

Bettys

Bradford

Leeds

A1

CAFE TEA ROOMS

Bettys

Illustration by David Hobbs

47

Bettys Harrogate

From the swathes of crocuses which herald the spring, through to the autumn colours, the Stray is always a delight, and a window table at Bettys is the best place to enjoy it.

Harrogate is a treat to visit at any time of year. It is a floral town of great repute, with the 200-acre Stray parkland making what must be the biggest municipal front garden in Europe.

One of my abiding childhood memories is the excitement each October when the fairy lights in scores of Stray trees would be switched on. Fifty years later, the Stray illuminations are still a stylish spectacle every evening throughout the winter months.

It takes well over 170 staff to keep Bettys Harrogate open seven days and evenings a week. You'll see a lot of them sporting Bettys brooches: bronze for ten years' service, silver for twenty years, gold for thirty. It's a family affair, too, with several mothers and daughters and sons working together.

The young students you see working here aren't hired casuals. Typically they are with us for six years, helping to pay their way through school and university. They receive the same professional training as full-time staff. Some just can't bear to leave us; the rest set out into the big wide world with that bit of extra confidence, charm, capacity for hard work, and an eye for a good cake that only Bettys training brings!

In recent times we have opened the first floor 'Imperial Suite' where you can book a table for tea at weekends, or book the whole room for your own private party or event. The first person to book the room was my mother – for her eightieth birthday party.

You can't book a table down in the tea rooms, so you will find celebrities queuing like everyone else. There are exceptions, such as when HRH The Prince of Wales asked if he could stop by for tea; his security put their foot down!

However busy we are, the queue still moves fast. As Uncle drummed into his staff from the early days: *'The most expensive thing in our business is an empty table.'*

Our Verandah Café, for everything from Afternoon Tea to an evening meal

The Imperial Room, all set for a party

Our Montpellier Café Bar, for continental style counter service

Intricate marquetry and wood panelling gives our
downstairs Spindler Room a cosy feel

Bettys at RHS Garden Harlow Carr

Teaming up with the Royal Horticultural Society to open a Bettys at their beautiful gardens on the south-western outskirts of Harrogate is our most recent addition.

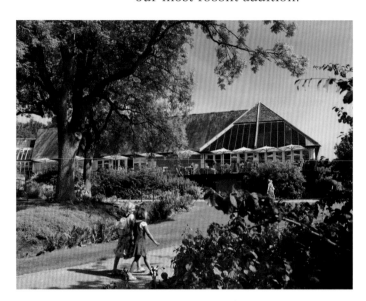

Ever since Lesley opened her Cookery School to provide opportunities for children to learn about real cooking, I have been searching for a partner for a similar project to enable children to learn about fruit and vegetables. That's how the conversation with the RHS started, and hopefully our educational kitchen garden will come to fruition. In the meantime we have created a stylish shop and café from which you can enjoy the lovely views whether or not you visit the garden itself.

Would Uncle approve of a Bettys in a garden? The Belmonts had a lovely garden but, unlike my parents and me, they were not 'hands-on' gardeners. They had a gardener called Spink. From his potting shed I salvaged a mirror advertising Jeyes Fluid, the disinfectant much beloved by old gardeners. Old Norman Brogden of Tockwith, who taught me how to grow vegetables, always drenched young carrot plants with Jeyes Fluid to put the root-fly off the scent. I dutifully tried it. It prevented an infestation but the carrots reeked of Jeyes. That was what sent me organic!

Each Bettys has a different feel to it, reflecting the location and the building. At Harlow Carr, Lesley and her team have created a Bettys fit for an English country garden.

Harlow Carr was created in 1950 by northern gardeners as a place to trial plant varieties for their suitability in the challenging Yorkshire climate. Today it is a charming pleasure garden of over sixty-five acres for armchair gardeners as well as keen horticulturists. No matter if you get lost in its gardens: in a distant corner is another Bettys – a little wooden tea house offering simple refreshments through the warmer months.

The light and airy Café befits a garden Bettys

Our Coffee Shop has a view of the garden you can enjoy rain or shine

Bettys Ilkley

Ilkley is many people's favourite Bettys. Blessed with a lovely Wharfedale location, the shop looks south towards Ilkley Moor and the café north towards Middleton Moor. In between the two views is a team of eighty of the most friendly, professional Bettys staff you are likely to meet.

If one or two of the youngsters are concentrating so hard they can barely smile, please forgive them. Learning the 'Bettys way' of doing things requires exacting training... and practice, practice, practice. Even the simplest task, such as laying up a tea tray, has five pages of precise detail in the training book. With experience these details become second nature, and the smile gets bigger and bigger.

Like Harrogate, Ilkley is a spa town with a real country feel. Its myriad of small independent shops are a good reason to visit the town for the day. More than anything else though, Ilkley is a place to walk!

The riverside and the lower reaches of Ilkley Moor were tamed with good paths in Victorian times. Beyond are the crags and the famous Cow and Calf rocks. A group of us from Bettys once set out to prove our Yorkshire grit by abseiling down the overhanging cliff of the Cow. Never again!

More my cup of tea are the wild moors that stretch beyond, both to the north and to the south of the town. You can even walk all the way to Harrogate, fifteen miles away, on high ground. Breakfast at one Bettys, high tea at the other, with a great day's walking in between. I know it can be done; I've done it myself! But please don't forget to leave your muddy boots at the door!

Our Café is as popular with local families as it is with visiting walkers

A good place to stock up on supplies before tackling the moors

TEA MERCHANTS & COFFEE ROASTERS

This impressive counter reminds us that tea and coffee, and the
traditions that go with them, are at the heart of our business

Bettys Northallerton

My father moved Bettys from Leeds here to the county town of North Yorkshire in 1971 when life in the city became too fraught and expensive.

His new premises were cosy but cramped, with not enough room for the queues. Thirty-three years later Lesley spotted the potential of a semi-derelict listed Georgian building nearby, and, after a year of restoration, the new Bettys opened in 2005.

On opening day we were all as excited as Uncle was back in July 1919 when the first Bettys opened in Harrogate.

Bettys Northallerton is as beautiful, as elegant, and as cosy as Uncle would have wished, with a Palm Room and an outdoor garden courtyard as well as the traditional tea room. In the shop is a coffee bar where coffee, cakes, and sandwiches are served to those in more of a hurry.

Northallerton certainly is a bustling town, with a thriving market taking over the high street in front of Bettys on Wednesdays and Saturdays and with other family businesses to provide a welcome respite from chain outlets.

Of course Northallerton is worth visiting in its own right, but it is also on the way to...well, everywhere! A perfect end to a day in Wensleydale or Swaledale to the west, or a start to a day on the North York Moors or Whitby on the coast to the east. Being only a few miles from the A1, Bettys Northallerton is a welcoming antidote to a motorway service station on any long journey to the north or south.

One trip to Northallerton, and I think Uncle would forgive and even congratulate us for closing his Leeds café and moving here, just as he would applaud us for moving out of Bradford to the country air of Ilkley.

Quite the suntrap in summer!

Elegant skylights ensure the Café is always beautifully bright

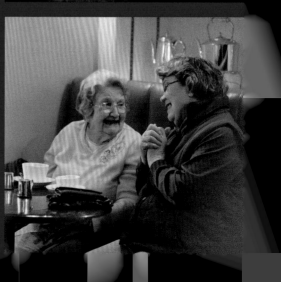

Bettys York

The city of York has so much history, and however long we are here, Bettys will always feel like a newcomer.

We occupy a privileged position right by the Lord Mayor's Mansion House. Across St Helen's Square, for the first forty years of its life, Bettys faced its great rival, Terry's Restaurant. Terry's had already been there for over 100 years before my great-uncle arrived in town, and many citizens thought Bettys an upstart. Only when Terry's closed in 1980 did Bettys become accepted as the place to meet in York. A weighty responsibility for us in such an important city.

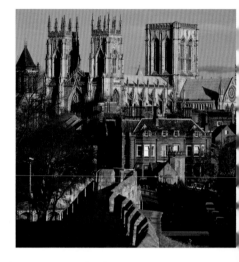

With such wonderful monuments and museums, it takes a week to see everything. When you are ready for refreshment, head for Bettys; it is never far away.

The ground-floor tea room is a very public place, somewhere to watch the world go by through the elaborate stained-glass windows, or, as night falls, listen to the café pianist.

The basement Oakroom has stained glass too, but is most notable for its oak panelling, which must have witnessed many a saucy wartime assignation in the days when it was Bettys Bar. In a corridor is the original 1940s' wartime mirror with its 500 etched signatures of servicemen, mostly Canadian aircrew.

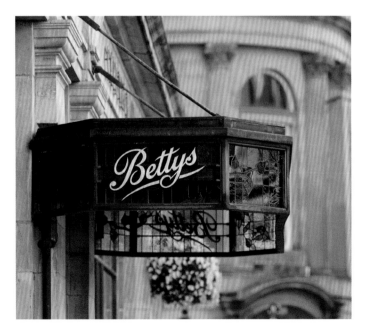

Upstairs, the art deco Belmont Room is unchanged since the *Queen Mary* days, and can be booked for private events.

Yes, memories abound in York. Alan is the longest-serving member of staff. I worked under him when he was head chef in the 1970s. Nowadays he works front of house as *maître d'*, and is the one to ask about the old days.

The ghost of Mrs Belmont is sighted from time to time. Why she prefers Bettys York I cannot explain, but she keeps everyone in good order!

'Somewhere to watch the world go by'

Afternoon Tea upstairs in the
Belmont Room

Our downstairs Oakroom

Our busy shop, where tourists seek out that must-have Bettys
souvenir alongside locals popping in for their 'daily bread'

Little Bettys, York

Maybe because it's by far the oldest Bettys building, maybe because it is in historic Stonegate right opposite a snickleway called 'Coffee Yard', Little Bettys has the strongest feel of the old eighteenth-century coffee house about it.

Those London coffee houses were called 'penny universities' because they were great schools of conversation, wit, and learning, and the entrance fee was only a penny.

Long before it became Little Bettys, No. 46 Stonegate was called the Georgian Tearooms. Sixty years ago it was owned by a Mr and Mrs Dick. Mr Dick was a shadowy figure who could be glimpsed standing by the big boiler in the kitchen. Mrs Dick busied herself serving tea and coffee at the ground and first-floor tables. Every now and then a young man – sometimes two or three – would enter and disappear straight upstairs to the second floor. A bell would ring and Mrs Dick would climb the stairs with a trayful of coffee and toasted teacakes. This was York's 'penny university', a private club for the intellectual élite of Nunthorpe Grammar School. They would discuss Shakespeare, the Classics in translation (even occasionally texts in Latin), and other less exalted topics, and every now and then pull a rope to ring the bell to summon Mrs Dick with more refreshments. John Langton, the well-known York artist, was a member of this club in the late 1940s and told me the story.

In the 1960s the new university in York provided a fresh intellectual clientele; obviously very fresh indeed, because since that era the cosy room at the back of the café has been known as 'Lovers' Corner'!

Little Bettys still has university links and it's not unusual to see a professor or two taking tea. Lesley gives a lot of her time to support and advise the University of York, and is one of its three Pro-Chancellors.

The first floor Café has great views of the bustling medieval street below

Lovers' Corner

Behind the Scenes at the Tea Rooms

There is more going on behind the scenes at a Bettys tea room than you can imagine. With as many as 170 staff per tea room, back-of-house is like a small village. However, it is not like the 'below stairs' of the old days.

Service is not servitude, and our staff have come to expect to have as pleasant facilities as their customers. Free food and drinks, newspapers, and internet help them relax and recharge their batteries. Serving your needs is mentally and physically demanding, but you rarely hear anyone letting off steam behind the scenes. It really is a friendly place; everyone says it's the best bit about working at Bettys.

Peep through the kitchen doors, and you will see gleaming modern kitchens; our practices are rather old-fashioned though. Lesley has never allowed microwave ovens in our kitchens; if things need cooking, they get cooked the time-honoured way, in pans or under grills. Proper food deserves proper respect, Lesley argues. We see ourselves as cooks, not chefs, and it is in the art of wholesome cooking that we train our staff.

However much we all clean as we go, we still need a team of housekeepers to tidy up after us. As if they weren't busy enough already, what with aprons to iron, silverware and brassware to polish, and cloakrooms to service.

Can you imagine how many items our dishwashing team wash on a busy Saturday? Over 7,000 at Bettys Harrogate alone! It's the one department where service does sometimes feel like servitude! I know from my own experience.

Peeping through our kitchen doors...

Every morning our drivers arrive at each Café with the day's supply of freshly baked treats

Not a microwave in sight!

Bettys Cookery School

Lesley was outraged! As an A-stream student in the 1960s she had been denied cookery classes, but the thought that practical cookery skills had now been more or less sidelined from the whole of the national school curriculum was too much to bear.

Are there many other life skills as important as being able to cook for yourself, simply, safely, and cheaply? It was 2001 and time to make a dream come true. She would open a cookery school. Local schools could use it for free, the paying public would be taught by our own experts, and our staff could enjoy a training facility second to none.

The school has been a great success. Although it looks dauntingly professional with eighteen workstations and a demonstration 'theatre', the atmosphere is so relaxed that the beginner and the experienced, the teenager and the granny work happily side by side.

Lesley's first attempt to teach cookery was thirty years ago in France when she showed her friend Beatrice how to make Yorkshire puddings. Using French ingredients, it was a disaster! Little did Lesley know that she had left one Yorkshire pudding in the back of the oven. Returning the following year we found a charred black object nailed to the kitchen wall. An inscription on the wall (politely translated here) ran: 'Fine example of typical English cooking.'

On that visit Beatrice served a less than perfect tarte tatin. Lesley resolved to become better than the French at this tricky dessert. Two decades later, she must make the best tarte tatin in the world. If you are lucky enough to be on a course when she is demonstrating it, you are in for a treat.

But you can taste Lesley's cooking anytime you like! The first print run of her cookery book *A Year of Family Recipes* sold out in no time, and we are well into the next run, so it's not just me who thinks it is brilliant.

Above all, cooking should be fun

Even the utensils must meet Bettys standards!

A watched pot...

The demonstration 'theatre' is an ideal way to learn from our experts

Bettys Craft Bakery

Half close your eyes for just a moment, and you could be in Switzerland not Harrogate. A Swiss chalet of a bakery, troughs of geraniums... and an ancient cowbell in the foyer to ring for attention.

The Bread and Pastry Rooms

Bakers working off bread doughs on wooden tables, and shaping pastries on a great marble slab. A wood-fired oven, not a flimsy metal slab-framed one that you might see in a pizzeria but a mighty one, insulated with ten tons of river sand maintaining a soothing evenness of heat that bakes a loaf to crusty perfection.

Perfection? Not quite. Every day, every loaf is ever so slightly different: a sign that humans and not machines are in control. Of course Bettys bakers have the best of technology: mixers, computer-monitored provers, and so on; but as with 100 years ago, it is the baker and not his tools that makes or breaks the bread.

Johann Bützer, my great-grandfather, might recognise the hefty Swiss Breakfast Loaves and Fitness Bread but he would be bemused by the Yorkshire Cobbles, Mouse Bread, and Fat Rascals, a fusion of two baking traditions that seems perfectly natural to my generation.

Brown paper and string might seem old-fashioned but there's no better way to insulate our slow-baked fruit cakes

Bid my bread feed
and my fire warm me

Marion has hand-decorated over a million

The Chocolate and Confectionery Rooms

In this part of the bakery, away from the ovens and the smell of baking, the eyes take over from the nose. Even the heady aroma of melted chocolate is barely noticed as visitors look in awe at craftsmanship which, around most of the world, died out decades ago.

At 6am the confectioners are finishing all the fresh cream cakes and fresh fruit flans, a race against time to be ready for the van-departure deadline of 7.30am. Then it's on to all the different fancies, which have to be produced in stages over two or three days. Often they start out as huge slabs, only taking shape in the final stages.

According to the seasons the confectioners can find themselves making deliciously sweet apples, carrots, pumpkins and pigs, Santas and snowmen. Meanwhile the cake-decorating team make every conceivable kind of flower by hand to adorn wedding cakes and Easter eggs: sweet peas, pansies, violets and lilies, brambles, roses, and daffodils. It's the edible country garden of every child's dreams.

Come rain or shine, the Chocolate Room is held at a constant temperature of 18°C. Chocolate is like a naughty child: having coaxed and cajoled it into good 'temper', all smooth and glossy with a crisp snap, you only have to turn your back for a moment for it to lose its temper and go grainy, blotchy, and 'bloomy'. Susceptible to heat and cold, draughts and damp, the only way to get chocolate to behave is to give it no excuse to misbehave! A constant 18°C does the trick.

The artistry does not end here: the chocolate-packing team are craftspeople too, tying ribbons and bows with mesmerising dexterity, and wearing white cotton gloves to polish Bettys golden guineas to perfection.

Then there are the fillings: praline, caramel, fresh cream, and champagne, delicate flavours which do not overpower the palate, all piped carefully by hand. Bettys chocolates must be good for you: just look at how healthy and slim the chocolatiers are!

In the 1920s, Uncle used to advertise Bettys chocolates as a slimming aid and a cure for weak hearts!

1929

Painstakingly decorating our elaborate Chocolate Ruffle Cake

A fine coating of raspberry dust gives our Champagne Truffles a lovely colour

Hand-piping 'Sarah Bernhardts'

Handmade from start to finish

Bettys by Post

I would love to be able to take Uncle to visit our mail-order department, Bettys by Post. I know he would be thrilled to see his dream come true – at last.

Uncle had always offered a mailing service at Bettys shops, but in 1935 he decided to set up a serious mail-order chocolate business. *'We have sent out 5,000 circulars'*, he wrote in his diary. The result of the mail shot was *'disappointing; about thirty orders'*. The first envelope he opened contained a postal order for 18/3d. The second contained a request for 3d. *'No stamp on the envelope… rather humorous… I wonder what will become of this department?'* See for yourself, Uncle! You were simply ahead of your time!

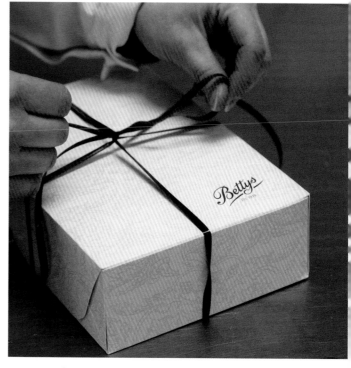

Seventy-five years later it's a thriving department with twenty-five staff, despatching orders all over the world. Almost half of the orders are nowadays received over the internet. We still prefer the personal contact when our customers phone us up!

Bettys by Post despatches over 45,000 parcels a year, from £100 hampers to small but regular supplies of tea and coffee to homesick Yorkshire souls in foreign parts, from Southend to Sydney.

Christmas is our busiest time with at least 100 products to choose from in our festive catalogue. But birthdays occur 365 days a year, and celebration cakes, chocolate tortes, and children's party cakes are despatched every day. When you get a parcel from Bettys by Post, you know someone thinks you are very special!

1928

We've even turned packing into an art form!

Our stock room, an Aladdin's Cave of Bakery treasures

Our high standards apply to how we answer

Taylors of Harrogate

Is there the faintest of aromas of apples and pears in your tea? For me there always will be, because when my father decided to move the newly acquired Taylors tea and coffee warehouse and roastery to Harrogate, he felled Bettys Bakery's orchard to make room for it.

I sense the orchard as a presence still haunting Plumpton Park – the site Bettys Bakery, Taylors of Harrogate, and Bettys Cookery School share to this day.

In the old warehouse in Leeds, back in Charles Taylor's day, they would handle 4,000 sacks, chests, and barrels of tea and coffee a year. Today we import nearly 200,000 a year. It takes a team of over 300 staff to buy, blend, roast, pack, and distribute it.

The list of tropical countries and islands we import from whets the appetite for an exotic holiday: India, Sri Lanka, China, Japan, Kenya, Ethiopia, Rwanda, Burundi, Tanzania, South Africa, Brazil, Colombia, Peru, Costa Rica, Nicaragua, Guatemala, Mexico, Cuba, Jamaica, Java, and Sumatra, each producing their own unique-tasting beverage according to the soil, the climate, the harvesting method, and the strain of plant.

It seems like very hard work, but all these countries have to be visited... regularly! It takes a team of ten buyers to share the burden, but this direct personal contact with the growers of our tea and coffee is crucial. Without it there is no mutual trust and understanding, no opportunity to secure the pick of the crop, no way of establishing realistic, ethical, fair trading relationships.

We don't just pay top prices to be charitable: it is all about rewarding quality and recognising growers who are dedicated to putting in the extra effort and attention to detail. In these circumstances it's a pleasure to pay the best prices and present much-appreciated enamel 'Rewarding Quality' plaques.

For many years I felt we were a lone voice in wanting to encourage good ethical and environmental practices on tea and coffee farms. Indeed I insisted that our buyers qualified as social auditors and appointed a full-time ethical trading manager.

Nowadays there is a much more collaborative approach throughout the tea and coffee trade and many farms have joined together to work with certification organisations like the Rainforest Alliance, The Fairtrade Foundation and Utz, each of whom have particular strengths in particular countries.

Our own 'stamp of approval' is still the most important to us, and we would rather support a top-quality farm that hasn't yet been officially certified, than put a 'badge' on a packet just for the sake of being seen to be 'Fairtrade'.

It's all about personal contact and relationships, trusting in our own eyes – and taste buds!

Tea buyer Simon in Assam, presenting our 'Rewarding Quality' plaque

Picking coffee in Sumatra

Coffee buyer Hannah visits a Nicaraguan school part-funded
by the premiums we pay for our coffee

Trainee tea-buyer Suzy spent months overseas
helping our growers perfect their tea

When they are not travelling our buyers have even more serious work to do. The two tasting rooms – one for tea, one for coffee – are the homes of extraordinary skill, creativity, and craftsmanship.

There is the discipline and concentrated effort of tasting up to 900 teas a day, judging quality, detecting faults, looking for nuances of character, body, colour, and flavour, and assessing their potential to brew better in either hard or soft water.

There is the skill of putting together blends, for the perfect cup of tea or coffee is often a complex blend of different origins, each one selected to bring a particular characteristic to the whole. As the seasons change in different parts of the world, so must the components of our blends change, and yet you, our customer, must get your favoured flavour consistently throughout the year.

Then there is the creativity of inventing new blends. Although we are a very traditional business, we thrive on the stimulus of new ideas. I think that creating blends successfully depends on wisdom rather than cleverness. There is no substitute for years (and years) of training to develop the deep knowledge and understanding of these extraordinary tropical commodities.

Back in 1962 when he took over the tiny Taylors tea and coffee business, my father had no idea that fifty years later our buying skills would be in such demand. It was never really our intention, but the public's appreciation for what we do has taken our Taylors products far beyond Bettys.

Our Yorkshire Tea is the nation's best-selling top-quality tea, and similarly our roast and ground coffees set the quality standard for the coffee market. We export to twenty-five countries including the USA, Australia, Canada, Japan, and across Europe.

I have to confess that Yorkshire Tea nearly wasn't called Yorkshire. When the printer's proofs of the first packaging were shown to the directors, they all nodded their approval and it was duly minuted. It was only after the meeting that an error was spotted by our tea-buying director, Warren Ford, the best tea man of his generation. On all six faces of the box, 'Yorkshire' was spelt without the 'k'. I doubt 'Yorshire Tea' would have proved so popular. In fact, it would have been a monumental disaster.

However successful we are, we will never be the biggest, but our buying team will always strive to be the best. We always keep some of our rarest finds exclusively for Bettys and Bettys by Post. You can always be assured of ordering a pot of something in our café which literally no one else in the world will be drinking. That's a nice feeling.

Meanwhile, if you fancy a career with our buying team it does help to be able to ride a horse, as buyer Kate once found in Peru, when horseback was the only way to get to a remote coffee farm which had never had a visitor before.

Our coffee buyers taste hundreds of coffees to check everything from the quality of the beans to the way they are roasted

When tea tasting, we also inspect the brewed leaves - not to read the future, but because it is an important indication of the quality!

Our tea and coffee factory is like no factory you would imagine. Ours is no gloomy place. There are huge windows everywhere to let the sunshine in, and to give views out into a lush subtropical garden and our Tropical House, where we raise coffee, tea, and cocoa plants.

Blending a dozen different teas together, a ton at a time, is a gentle process. A large drum tumbles the teas in just eight slow rotations, so the leaf is not damaged. Teas with flowers and scents are blended in much smaller batches, and very special teas are inspected almost leaf by leaf before they end up on the tea counter at Bettys.

Nowadays, most people want their tea in convenient tea-bag form. In the Yorkshire Tea Hall, very clever machines (run by even cleverer engineers) pack the tea into bags, and thence into boxes, faster than you can blink.

Coffee has to be roasted as well as blended. We still use basically the same technology of a rotating drum with a gas flame that we used fifty, even 100, years ago. Of course, there is still a good, slow, even roast, with infinite possibilities to roast darker or lighter to suit the particular blend.

Although grinding coffee beans in your own kitchen creates an aroma almost as delectable as drinking the coffee itself, most people want the convenience of ready-ground coffee. Preserving the aroma is the most important thing and we have the best technology to do just that.

In our shops we grind beans straight into the bag; in the coffee hall we do just the same, but here flushing away all the air as we seal the coffee into airtight bags. Being so fresh, the coffee continues to give off roasting gases for some time and would explode the bag if it wasn't for the cunning little one-way valve on the front of the pack. It's the oxygen in the air that stales coffee and ruins the aroma, so always keep your coffee airtight and cool!

All this technology is a far cry from the early days. In my teenage years I could never understand how so many bits of my Meccano set went missing. When I joined the business and started training at Taylors I discovered that half the machines were held together with my Meccano! My father was his own chief engineer in those days.

Back in 1976, I remember spending weeks and weeks packing our first export order. It was for Egypt. Tens of thousands of packets of tea were labelled 'Camel Brand' in Arabic, and were then packed into chests tied with special straps so the merchants could attach them to camels and take them out into the desert to sell the tea to the nomads.

Life at Taylors is still an extraordinary whirl of importing and exporting. One or two things are home grown, though. The crop from our own Tropical House is very small, but a cup of Harrogate-grown coffee or tea is something really special. For those in the know, the Tropical House is a fitting monument to the memory of Uncle's orchard.

You pass by our Plumpton Park site on the train from Harrogate to York, just between Starbeck and the aptly named Belmont Crossing. Look out for a giant teapot clock. If your train is running exactly to time the clock is programmed to pour before your very eyes!

'Camel' teapot

'Huge windows everywhere to let the sunshine in'

How things have changed since the days when my Meccano
would go missing...

With this many shelves it pays to remember where
you put everything!

Inspecting the tea leaf by leaf to ensure the quality is right

A courtyard garden, complete with Tropical House

Trees for Life

It all started with a promise: the sort of vague, unfulfillable promise a parent sometimes makes to their children, and shouldn't. Except my promise wasn't vague: it was very, very precise.

I arrived home from work one day in autumn 1989 to find seven-year-old Chloë, and five-year-old Daniel in great distress. *Blue Peter* had been showing a film of a burning rainforest, wantonly destroyed and its inhabitants displaced to make way for industrial-scale cattle ranching.

'Don't worry' I said to my tearful children, *'we'll replant them. If you plant one tree here in Harrogate, I'll find a way to plant nine hundred and ninety-nine thousand, nine hundred and ninety-nine more.'*

Chloë and Daniel planted their tree on the Stray near Bettys, so I could see it from my office window. To make doubly sure I would not forget my rash promise, my colleagues carved a stone plaque with the words, 'Trees for Life, First of a Million' and placed it by the tree, a hornbeam.

The tree is still there, as is the plaque. A dozen paces to the west is a younger tree, an oak, with a stone plaque that reads 'Trees for Life, the millionth tree.'

I thought we could get to a million trees in one year. In fact it took ten, and it was a sixteen-year-old Daniel who posed for the cameras at the planting ceremony. We got there not just because of the financial commitment of the business, but because of the support of our customers. Loyal Yorkshire Tea drinkers, schools, and Women's Institutes all collected our 'tree tokens' year after year after year after year.

We have been involved with many tree planting projects in the UK, including our own 'Babes in the Wood' forest in the Yorkshire Dales, where we planted a tree for every child or grandchild born to a member of staff.

But the main thrust of our efforts has been working in the tropics with charities like Oxfam, where if we help communities set up tree nurseries and plant trees on sufficient scale, we can quickly transform the land and even make it rain again. As the head woman of an Ethiopian village said to a group of visiting staff and WI members, *'Before, the land was dry and useless, now it is green and where there is green there is hope.'*

There are two more 'Trees for Life' trees you can look out for in Harrogate. Right outside Bettys is the two millionth tree, planted by HRH The Prince of Wales in 2003, and up at Harlow Carr is the three millionth, planted in 2008. It is called the 'Blue Peter' tree for good reason. When the children's programme heard what they had unwittingly started nineteen years previously, they sent a film crew and a presenter to help twenty-four-year-old Daniel plant the tree.

And, on camera, I made a new promise to my children: to get to the heart of the greatest environmental threat to the planet and its climate – rainforest destruction. Next, we will save a million trees, precious rainforest trees. But that's the next chapter.

Daniel, aged 5, with the tree that started it all

Daniel and me planting the three millionth tree –
with help from Blue Peter presenter Zöe Salmon

32,000 TREES planted thanks to YORKSHIRE TEA

With support from the ladies of the WI we planted a wood of 32,000 trees

Into the Future

July 17th, 2009. Another milestone. Our 90th birthday celebrations looked back with nostalgia.

We re-created Uncle's staff charabanc outings, re-enacting his 1921 trip to Whitby, this time taking over 500 staff and their families for a day at the seaside. As in our Diamond Jubilee year, we recreated cakes and dishes from our archives, held concerts and dinners, and most important of all, completed the refurbishment and extension of Bettys Harrogate – the first to be opened but the last to be re-equipped to twenty-first-century standards. But still no microwaves!

But, however cosy Bettys appears, the challenges of the next decade come from the wider world. The ritual of Bettys – the tea, the coffee, the chocolate – is founded on the climate rhythms of the tropics. And the rhythms are changing before our eyes.

It's either raining too much, or not at all. Deforestation not only reduces rainfall but the resulting soil degradation means that when it does rain rapid run-off leads to flooding hundreds of miles downstream.

Replacing precious rainforest with industrial-scale agriculture is not going to work. Our mission, on your behalf and on behalf of future generations of your family, is to take what action we can in the next decade to help indigenous peoples save what remains of the most endangered tracts of rainforest in the tropics.

We are a small Yorkshire business but we need to think big. We have committed to support rainforest protection projects equivalent in size to Yorkshire itself. That's 1.5 million hectares of forest. We are starting with a Rainforest Foundation project in the Peruvian Amazon, where the Ashaninka tribal homeland is 237,000 hectares, just slightly larger than the size of the Yorkshire Dales National Park.

Whilst we are funding work on healthcare, community organisation and advocacy skills, mapping and forestry skills, we have a particular interest in helping develop high-quality coffee and cocoa growing on a community rather than an industrial scale. This will enable the Ashaninka to fund their own development in the long term, whilst we move onto other rainforest projects.

The response from our customers to all our fund-raising initiatives has been extraordinary so far and if this continues we will be able to provide the £750,000 needed. In the meantime, the money raised from sales from the first edition of this book have gone to fund the planting of an educational temperate forest at Harlow Carr around our three millionth 'Blue Peter' tree. It will be a forest you can live in, and live off, and remind future generations how much earlier generations understood about living with forests without destroying them. We are using ancient wisdom and practices, such as bringing in pigs to clear the land of brambles and weeds. In a few years it will be an important educational feature of the RHS garden at Harlow Carr, to remind us that without trees, there is no life.

'Without trees...'   '...there is no life'

So remote are the Ashaninka lands that an eight-hour boat trip down the River Ene is the only way to reach the nearest town

Cocoa, cultivated sustainably, could provide Ashaninka communities with the means to support themselves

CHAPTER 3

The Treasures of Bettys

The Treasures of Bettys
Marquetry

Uncle spent far too much money on his premises in his efforts to create what in his adverts he called: *'surroundings with the quiet harmony of perfect taste'*. On display at Bettys Harrogate and Ilkley is his collection of exquisite marquetry pictures from the studio of Charles Spindler in Alsace, France.

Charles Spindler founded his studio in the late 1890s at the height of the art nouveau period. Instead of using marquetry just to make pretty floral pictures on furniture, he used natural unstained veneers, collected from around the world, to create literally 'paintings in wood'.

His son, Paul, an equally talented artist and craftsman, joined him in the studio in the early 1920s. Paul's son, Jean-Charles, followed suit in the 1970s and still runs the studio in the tiny village of St Leonard, surrounded by vineyards against the backdrop of the forested Vosges mountains.

When Uncle discovered Spindler's work in the early 1930s he bought a few pieces for his own 'den' at home. In 1934 he commissioned the studio to make six large pictures of Yorkshire scenes to hang in Bettys Harrogate. Young Paul Spindler travelled over and drew the sketches from which the evocative pieces that hang in the Harrogate 'Spindler Room' were made.

Lesley and I made contact with the family again in 1976 and over the years added to his collection, including the largest marquetry picture ever made in the studio, *La Chasse* ('The Hunt') – which hangs in Bettys Ilkley.

Fountains Abbey

Ripon

Burnt Yates

Bolton Abbey

Knaresborough

La Chasse

Jean-Charles serves us tea at his home in St Leonard

Spindler

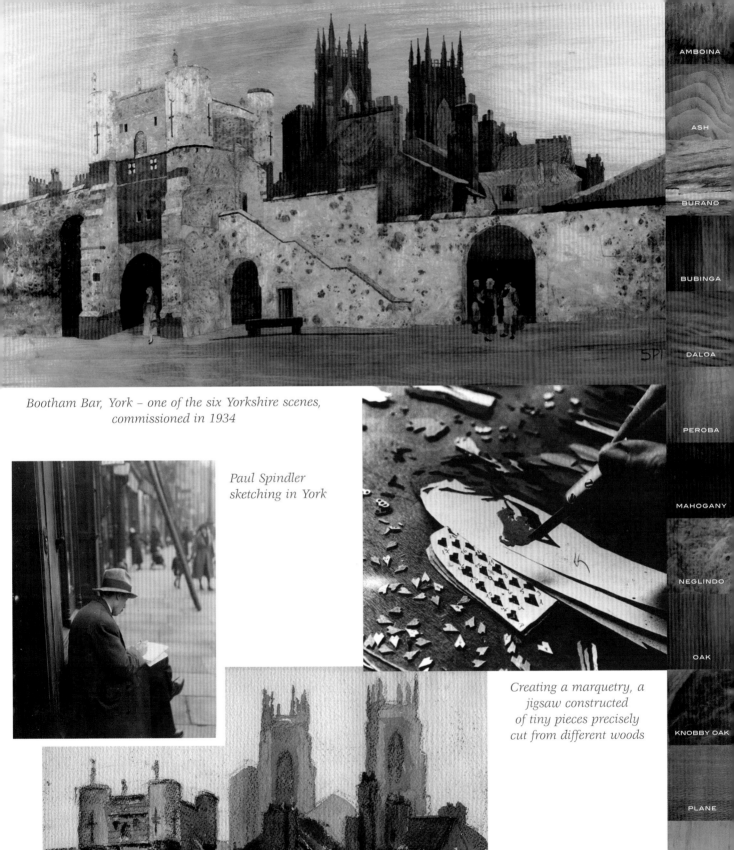

Bootham Bar, York – one of the six Yorkshire scenes,
commissioned in 1934

Paul Spindler
sketching in York

Creating a marquetry, a
jigsaw constructed
of tiny pieces precisely
cut from different woods

The initial sketch
of York

AMBOINA

ASH

BURANO

BUBINGA

DALOA

PEROBA

MAHOGANY

NEGLINDO

OAK

KNOBBY OAK

PLANE

POPLAR

TAMARIND

Teapots

'Patent Self-Pourer'

'Cadogan'

'Musical'

'Women's Institute'

'Simple Yet Perfect'

'Empire Clock'

'Cunard Cube'

'Battle of Trafalgar'

We have been collecting teapots at the rate of twenty a year for the last twenty-five years. The odd chip or restoration doesn't worry us: we do like a bargain, and there's no point having a collection which is too precious to be displayed.

My mother, Kay, has found many of the teapots in the collection, which ranges from 1750 to the present day.

We particularly seek out strange inventions, like the Earl of Dundonald's 'Simple Yet Perfect' pot, patented in 1901, which enables you to tilt the pot on its side after five minutes to separate the tea infusion chamber from the brew.

Then there is J. J. Royle's 'Patent Self-Pourer' of 1886, which enables the genteel hostess to pour the tea without lifting the teapot, by means of a cunning pump concealed in the lid.

We have several 'Cadogan' teapots, attributed to Lady Cadogan who in the 1830s liked to amuse her guests with a teapot with no visible means of getting the tea into the pot: it was filled through the base!

For music lovers there is the 'Musical' teapot, which plays whenever the pot is lifted, while for travellers there is the 'Empire Clock' teapot: by swivelling the lid you can tell what time it is in any part of the British Empire.

The Cunard steamship company devised the 'Cube', a teapot whose rebated handle and spout would survive any storm.

For Women's Institutes there is a pot with two spouts to deal with a thirsty queue all the quicker.

There is one we don't have – and which I have never seen – which was patented in 1812 by one Sarah Guppy, the wife of a Bristol merchant. An egg is suspended in a casket inside the pot so that by the time your tea is brewed, your breakfast egg is boiled! If you've got one let me know – please!

Animals abound in our collection – my favourites are the 'Minton Monkey' and the 'Panda' – as do commemoratives from the Battle of Trafalgar to the present.

'Emily Pankhurst'

Our collection of caricatures and satirical teapots includes 'Emily Pankhurst', who reminds me of my great aunt Liseli, who was a Swiss suffragette. The first teapot I ever bought was a Greatbach 'Prodigal Son'. Once addicted, the teapot I really, really wanted was a very rare caricature of Oscar Wilde, one of the nicknames I had to endure at school! It is called the 'Aesthetic'. My mother heard that one of these was up for auction by Sotheby's in Sussex. We had never paid anything remotely like £1,000 for a teapot before, but that is what I gave her to secure this gem. On the train down to Sussex she was joined in the compartment by a man who coincidentally was going to the same auction. He had never been to an auction before, but a friend of his, anxious to impress a girlfriend, wanted to obtain a particular piece of china for her and he had been given £6,000 in cash. My mother patiently explained to the novice how auctions worked and how to bid.

'Prodigal Son'

'Panda'

On arriving at the small country station, my mother found the taxi she had pre-booked. The man had made no such arrangements and there was no way he was going to get to the auction on time. Kay took pity on him and gave him a lift. In the taxi she asked him the question she knew she had to ask. 'Which piece of china are you bidding for?' She knew the answer before he replied. 'It's something called the "Aesthetic" – it's to do with Oscar Wilde.' Guess who got the teapot?

'Minton Monkey'

There is a happy ending. Hearing my mother's sad tale, a collector parted with his slightly chipped 'Aesthetic' at a knock-down price!

The two-faced slightly chipped 'Aesthetic'
with the reverse side cleverly reflected in a mirror

THE TREASURES OF BETTYS
Tea Prints and Paraphernalia

These girls are sorting the small tender leaves from the larger and coarser ones. It is tiresome work but the social occasion afforded is no little compensation

The sorted leaves are put on large bamboo trays placed in the sunshine to be dried and the long drying process begins. Both "green" and "black" tea are made from the same leaves only the drying process is different.

Little Bettys is the place to see examples from our large collection of prints, advertisements, and paraphernalia which tell the story of the tea trade.

Currently on display is a series of Japanese and Chinese prints. The most extraordinary one shows monkeys being used to pluck leaves from wild tea bushes on inaccessible crags. Another shows women using chopsticks to sort out the best leaves.

"Wake up and have a cup of Tea"

Carved ebony box presented to Edward, Prince of Wales, on his visit to Ceylon in 1875

'Sold to the man with more money than sense!'

The treasure that means the most to me is not on display. It brings back shameful memories.

It is the very last chest of tea sold in the London tea auction following its closure after 319 years of weekly auctions. London was for so long the most important auction in the world, but as the shift in tea consumption has moved to the Middle East, it is the auctions in the growing regions – Mombasa, Calcutta, Colombo, and Jakarta – that have taken over.

Our tea-buying team graciously awarded me the privilege of representing the company on this historic occasion on 29th June, 1998. Little did they realise that I would pay the highest price ever recorded for a single chest of tea: £18,315!

Fifteen companies started the bidding for the very last lot: one chest of *Hellbodde* Estate Ceylon Flowery Pekoe. By the time the price had escalated to £5,000, it was down to John Leeder of Twinings and myself. What with all the TV cameras and photographers there, I'm afraid 'auction fever' possessed me. Anyway, I was absolutely convinced that the rightful home for this treasure was in Yorkshire. It was all for charity, so how could I be blamed if I kept on bidding and bidding?

As penance, I have not bid in any kind of auction since! Correction: I have not been *allowed* to bid in any kind of auction since!

Can you imagine a pirate being awarded an MBE? Well, one has, and he works for us!

Captain Rummage, MBE (also known as Chris Powell) tours the region in full pirate uniform 'talking rubbish' with schools and social enterprises. At his 'trading post' he converts trash into tradeable treasure: craft materials, gardener's tools and playgroup toys, while raising funds for our Yorkshire Rainforest Project.

Chris has reduced considerably the amount of our waste going to landfill. Together with tree planting and our social and environmental projects on tea and coffee farms, his work has played a major part in our winning not just one, but two Queens Awards for Enterprise for Sustainable Development.

I took 'Captain Rummage' to Buckingham Palace to the Queen's reception for her award winners. Now, for a captain, Chris is a very sober pirate: he doesn't drink – not even rum or grog. So I was just a little concerned, waiting in a stateroom for our turn to pass down the receiving line and shake hands with HM the Queen, when he downed a glass of champagne in one. As soon as we had done our bowing Chris downed another glass and said: *'Thank goodness that's over.'* I didn't dare tell him it wasn't, that I had been tipped off by an equerry that the Queen wished to talk to us.

At least my other companion was sober. I had also taken with me Katy Squire, who had organised all our tree planting projects around the world for the past fifteen years. Katy was looking pale, tense, and unsteady. No wonder: she was seven months pregnant with twins! I had taken the precaution of advising the Palace in advance of her condition, but surely she wasn't going to give birth right now, here in the Palace? At that moment an equerry touched my arm and suddenly she was there, The Queen, all smiles and questions. Chris and Katy relaxed, and were great ambassadors. I was so proud… and relieved!

The oldest medal in our collection is a gold medal for coffee roasting won by Charles Taylor at the London Grocery Exhibition of 1896. The earliest-surviving medal won by Frederick Belmont was from the International Confectionery Exhibition of 1928, but we treasure more his 'passing out' certificate of 1903 from the Swiss Master Bakers' Association.

Since those days, although staff have won many awards for training, community and environmental achievements, it is the awards for outstanding craft skills and service, in the tradition of our founder, that mean most to us.

Our bakery team members have brought in a fine harvest of national medals for bread, pastry, and patisserie and our head confectioner, Helen Proudfoot, represented Great Britain in the WorldSkills Championships in Helsinki in 2005.

Not to be outdone, our café teams have won over fifty Awards of Excellence from the Tea Council and 'Top Tea Place of the year' on three occasions.

It has been a great boost to confidence to receive these awards over the years – and we treasure them dearly – but what makes us all most proud is the recognition we receive day after day from loyal customers who choose to spend their money with us. Now that's what we call praise!

Our most precious treasure of all is our heritage. Although we are now really a Yorkshire family, our Swiss heritage still has an enormous impact on the way the business is run. Whether it is Swiss products, Swiss techniques, or simply Swiss precision, finesse, and attention to detail, Switzerland still has a clear voice in our culture.

An arduous wine tasting in the vineyard

To keep that voice alive and resonant, staff attend courses at the Swiss Bakery School in Lucerne, and at the chocolate school run by Felchlin, a Swiss family business that sources all our cocoa beans for us and processes them into raw chocolate before shipping it for us to temper and craft into our silky smooth chocolates. From time to time Lesley has taken a group of staff to eat and drink their way round Switzerland. In the cities the group visit smart cafés, bakeries, and chocolate shops and go out to dinner with my Swiss cousin Nelli. In the mountains they make a pilgrimage to the wonderful Ruedihus in Kandersteg to taste traditional rustic dishes, or journey to Pontresina in the Engadine where my father trained after the war, and where the Kochendörfer and Walther families always make us welcome.

Sprüngli, Zürich

The Ruedihus

The mill at Wangen-an-der-Aare

Visiting the mill at Wangen-an-der-Aare where our family story begins is always emotional, but a tasting at the Bonvin family vineyard, from where we import all our Swiss wine, soon cheers everyone up.

Nearly 2,000 feet up, on a craggy outcrop overlooking the Rhone valley, surrounded by snow-capped mountains, this really is a vineyard with a difference. Mountain weather can be treacherous, but here in southern Switzerland the weather is perfect for vines, with long hot summers merging into autumn. It never

'A vineyard with a difference'

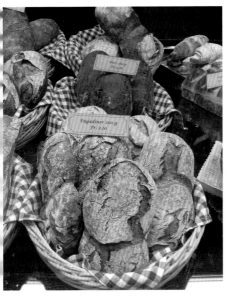

A Zürich shop window

gets too hot because at about two o'clock in the afternoon a cooling breeze starts to waft down the valley from the Rhône glacier at its head. The Bonvin wines we import are really too good, too special to be 'house wines', but we can't resist.

Switzerland draws heavily from the culture of its neighbours, Italy, France, Germany, and Austria, and we too stray over the borders in our influences.

Italy has always been a strong influence on us, and Lesley takes her groups south to Milan to visit Peck's food hall and the famous café Cova – which serves our tea! Whether it's Venetian festival cake, Sienese panforte, panettone, or rustic breads, we always go back to authentic recipes and then give them a Bettys twist, which we hope you'll agree makes them better than the mass-produced ones which are imported into this country.

That's enough travelling for now! I must admit that one of our dreams is to open a Bettys hotel in the Swiss mountains, so we can all take turns to work there for a month or two each year! Hmmm... maybe we should just stick to what we know we are good at.

Spot the site for Bettys...

A Bettys shop window

CHAPTER 4

Who Was Betty?

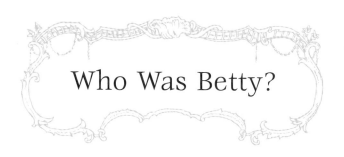

Who Was Betty?

1st August: today is Yorkshire Day, when we wear our white roses with extra pride. Seven hundred miles away on the same day the Swiss are celebrating Swiss National Day. On this day of double celebration for a Swiss-Yorkshire business, it seems a good time to enquire whether 'Betty' was Swiss or Yorkshire.

Whilst all our family plead ignorance, everyone else has their own theory about the elusive Betty. I receive letters on the subject quite regularly, always quite plausible accounts of how somebody's great-grandmother Elizabeth – or Lilibet if Swiss – was an intimate friend of Frederick Belmont a century ago.

One sentimental story claims that Frederick called Bettys after the daughter of the doctor who practised next door to the new café premises. The young girl was dying of TB and Frederick said he would immortalise her name forever.

Betty Lupton, 'Queen of the Wells'

The next story is almost too obvious to be true. The most famous character in the history of Harrogate was Betty Lupton. For nearly sixty years from 1778 Betty was in charge of dispensing the sulphur waters to visitors to the spa. She and her assistants were called 'ladlers' or 'nymphs'. Betty was known as 'Chief Nymph' until, in June 1838, on the very day of Queen Victoria's coronation, Betty herself was crowned 'Queen of the Harrogate Wells'. Did Frederick decide to endear himself to the Harrogate population by calling his café after their spa 'Queen'? We have in our collection Betty Lupton's own cup and saucer, passed on by one of her descendents who was convinced of the veracity of this tale.

Here are two much more likely stories. I have researched them thoroughly. They could be true; I would quite like them to be true. You decide.

A few years ago a lady telephoned to say that she had some gossip about Betty that she had been dying to tell me for years; only her mother had always forbidden her to divulge such tittle-tattle.

Back in the 1950s her family had moved to Harrogate and lived in lodgings owned by a Miss Firth. Miss Firth had revealed the secret to her mother.

Miss Firth, my Auntie Hilda! Not a real aunt but my great-aunt Bunny Belmont's best friend. My abiding memory of her is after Christmas dinner every year, when she would settle, just a little tipsy, in an armchair and start to recite from memory the Rubaiyat of Omar Khayyam, the epic poem.

Our challenge was to distract her as quickly as possible before she got into her stride and get her to play 'passing the matchbox from nose to nose' or 'relay racing with a balloon between the knees'.

Auntie Hilda almost appeared in an earlier chapter – 2nd October, 1952. Auntie Bunny was round at Auntie Hilda's having her usual Saturday pre-lunch Martini at the very moment when Dickie Belmont had his heart attack. At that same moment my mother was pushing my sister and me in our pram down Otley Road to visit Auntie Hilda.

Betty Balfour

Betty Howe

Is Auntie Hilda destined to take centre stage now? Her explanation of the Bettys mystery is quite simple. Around about 1915 there had been a London musical called *Betty*! Frederick had seen the show and taken a real shine to its leading lady, called Betty. Auntie Hilda did not suggest that a relationship ensued; simply that is why a few years later he called his new venture 'Bettys'.

The play *Betty* seemed to have sunk without trace: I could find no evidence of its existence, although I found a number of glamorous actresses of the period called Betty, including one – Betty Fairfax – whose publicity photos were taken by a photographer in Harrogate. Was she the elusive Betty who caught the rascally roving eye of my great-uncle?

Betty Bronson

The most famous celebrity baby of the time was also a Betty, and I have a dozen publicity postcards of 'Baby Betty', the daughter of the actors Ellaline Terriss and Seymour Hicks. She is cute, but surely not the face that launched a tea shop empire?

Betty Fairfax

Two years later I tracked the play down at Bristol University's Theatre Collection. The more I learnt about the play, the more I realised why Frederick Belmont might have been drawn to this story of a humble servant girl who, through love, finds a place in society; a reflection of his own life story, perhaps?

Betty Blythe

Little Betty Hicks

"BETTY"

A Musical Play in Three Acts
By FREDERICK LONSDALE
and GLADYS UNGER.

Music by
PAUL A. RUBENS.

Additional Numbers by
ERNEST STEFFAN and
MERLIN MORGAN

Lyrics by
ADRIAN ROSS and
PAUL A. RUBENS.

The Play produced by
EDWARD ROYCE.

MR. GEORGE EDWARDES.

I discovered that the impresario George Edwardes had put on *Betty* at Daly's Theatre in London, first night 24th April, 1915. D. Forbes Wilmslow, the theatre historian, wrote:

'Cinderella is the oldest plot in musical comedy. "Find a new twist in it," stage people say, "and there is a fortune." In spite of innumerable adaptations made by so many authors, its sweet simplicity still finds interested audiences and sympathetic readers. Betty, a beautiful play set to charming music, exploits the sentiments of the Cinderella theme. It ran for 391 performances. A simpler or more tender little love piece was never produced at Daly's – that is the highest tribute I can pay to the charms of Betty.'

The twist in this tale is that this Cinderella is very badly treated by her prince. The Duke of Crowborough tells his wayward only son, Gerard, that he will disinherit him if he doesn't marry and settle down. In a fit of pique Gerard proposes to one of the kitchen maids, Betty, who accepts him and he tells her she must be ready to be married on the morrow. Next morning Gerard marries Betty, who carries herself like a princess; but still he rudely packs her off to the country and continues his wild bachelor life in London. The Duke is so incensed at his son's behaviour that he disinherits him and makes all his money over to Betty. After many more twists and turns *'the curtain drops on a very happy couple'.*

What makes Auntie Hilda's story all the more plausible was our discovery that the play came to Harrogate's Grand Opera House on no less than three occasions between 1916 and 1918. Was it just the story that attracted him, or was it one of the leading ladies? Did young Frederick Belmont fall for the charms of Miss Winifred Barnes, Miss Isobel Delorme, or Miss Nellie Taylor, all of whom starred as the young kitchen maid Betty?

MISS WINIFRED BARNES AS BETTY AND MASTER CYRIL DOUGHTY AS A PERT PAGE

Betty Rose

Now the other story. In 1987 my father received a letter from two ladies who claimed that their aunt – still alive – had always told them that she was the Betty in 'Bettys'. Winifred Elizabeth Rose was her name, or simply Betty Rose. The nieces wrote that Betty Rose was the granddaughter of the lady who really founded Bettys, and that young Betty had walked into the dining room at her grandmother's house where the new directors were trying to decide what to call their café venture. Instead of telling her off for interrupting their meeting, grandmother looked at the lovely young Betty carrying a toy tea tray and decided: 'We will call it Bettys!'

I went to visit Betty Rose, then in her eighties and living in the Cotswolds. Unfortunately Betty could not recall the famous occasion itself, even though she would have been eleven or twelve at the time. It was her mother who always told her that Bettys was named after her following this chance interruption. Betty Rose was such a lovely lady, and so proud of her association, that I just had to adopt her as my official Betty. What clinched it was the hand-tinted old photograph of her on her dining-room wall: a portrait of a lovely little girl carrying a tea service.

It was long after Betty Rose's death that, with the help of her nieces and our company archives, I pieced together the background to the Betty Rose story.

In his letter of 21st February, 1921, Frederick Belmont alluded to other shareholders; *'but I am the only one that understands the business'.* What he didn't say was that the crucial funding had come from his new wife's Aunt Mary. Mary Wood was the widow of a very successful Harrogate grocer and tea dealer, John Wood. After his death in 1904 she continued to run the business in James Street herself. The Woods were staunch Quakers who were renowned for their philanthropy. Mary's generosity extended to her niece and her ambitious Swiss husband. It was Mary Wood who paid the deposit on the first premises and guaranteed the mortgage. She had certain conditions attached to her generosity, though. Her two sons were to be directors along with her son-in-law Frederick Rose, who was a baker. She herself would be chairman of the board.

So Frederick Belmont was just one director surrounded by a tightly knit group of in-laws. Not for long, though: Mary Wood died in 1925, and her sons lost interest and sold their shares to another investor, a Leeds wine merchant. It was another five years before Frederick and Claire, now Dickie and Bunny, bought all the shares for themselves.

Actually, it was a bit more scandalous than that. In fact one of Mary's sons, George Wood, a solicitor, ceased to be a director on being jailed for purloining clients' money.

However rascally her sons, I like the sound of Mary Wood. From a faded family photograph my father has painted her portrait for the board room at Bettys. I can see her chairing that first meeting in her dining room at home at what is now the Mile Post Inn on Leeds Road. I can see twelve-year-old Betty bringing in the tea. I can hear Mary Wood saying 'We'll call it Bettys'. Could it be true? Unfortunately all the evidence is circumstantial. Perhaps that's for the best.

Bettys Tea Rooms were born of a love story – a romance between a young Swiss and his Harrogate landlady's daughter. It would be so appropriate if he had called the business after his bride.

Mary Wood

Many of her friends and staff from that era believe she is Betty. Her name, however, is Claire, and the only familiar name by which she was known was 'Bunny', as can be testified by the ladies of Pannal Golf Club, who compete annually for the 'Bunny Belmont Trophy'. No, it cannot be her, unless... An old friend of hers, Jimmy Ogden, once told my father that in her youth Bunny was a beautician and hairdresser and that her professional name was Betty. Unfortunately, I cannot verify that. She had her own 'salon' in a room above a florist and all the advertisements for it are in her own name, 'Claire Appleton'. Another theory bites the dust?

Actually, I quite like the thought that 'Bettys' could have been called 'Bunnys'! That would be infinitely preferable to 'Bettyfayre', a new name for Bettys proposed by some consultants in 1972.

Who can criticise us for staying loyal to Betty, whoever she may be?

The fact is that whenever my father asked his uncle 'Who was Betty?', Uncle changed the subject. *He did not want us to know.*

Bunny Belmont

The Bunny Belmont Trophy

Going through the Wood and Rose family archives I came across an entry Mary Wood had made in her daughter's visitors' book on 9th April, 1897:

There is no happiness like that of being loved by your fellow creatures and feeling that your presence is an addition to their comfort.

Mary Wood.

That would make a very good motto for Bettys. As an immigrant family the overwhelming desire always seemed to be not for riches but for acceptance and recognition by the community. Uncle truly relished being 'loved by his fellow creatures' and delighted in the thought that his creation – Bettys – was 'an addition to their comfort'.

What future generations will make of it all I do not know. The next book, which turns the work of my generation into sepia-tinted history will have to be written by the fourth generation of the family. Maybe they will see more clearly. Not too clearly, I hope; there is something reassuring and comforting about myths and legends, which can be spoiled by too much clarity. *He did not want us to know.*

If you have bought this book it must be because you know and love Bettys as a customer. Thank you. We will do our best to be around to serve your children and your children's children. I am sure they will still be asking the same old question: *'Just who was Betty?'*

'...'Scuse me miss, are you Betty?'

Thank yous

This book would have remained unwritten were it not for my editor, Sarah McKee. She worked in Bettys' shop in Ilkley for seven years, helping to pay her way through school, university, right through to her masters degree in history. She persuaded me to let her become our archivist for a year, and this book would not have been possible without her determination to put the company and family archives in good order. She has discovered photographs we didn't know we had, letters no one had got around to translating, and, above all, she charmed stories and anecdotes out of people renowned for their discretion and privacy.

Uncle always said: *'If we want something just right, we have to do it ourselves.'* True to his word we have designed and published this book ourselves. Thanks go to designers Georgina Gill, Jane Jardine, and Rebecca Watson for their work on the first edition, and to Dom Dwight and Laura Jukes, who edited and designed this second edition.

I would also like to give special thanks to:

Ruth Brock and Claire Cave, Bettys student archivists from 1998 to 2003,
and Dawn Taylor, keeper of the keys from 1980 to the present.

My mother, Kay Wild, and my Swiss Aunt Hanni, for photographs and memories.

Rodney Light for the lovely photograph of his late wife, Valerie Belmont.

Shirley Penfold, Claire Taylor, Mary Hodgson, and Harold Clarke
for Belmont mementoes and memories.

Ruth England and Jeanne Seagrove for photographs and memories of Betty Rose and Mary Wood.

The late Jim Raleigh, his late wife Muriel, and their godson Rixon Matthews, Helen Wrightson, Carole and Peter Topham, and the late Alison Taylor for photographs and memories of the Taylor family business.

The late Bill Baxter for entrusting us with Betty Lupton's cup and saucer.

The many staff who allowed us to 'snap' them at work.

The many retired staff who shared their memories of the old days.

The many photographers who have captured the spirit (but not the ghost) of present-day Bettys for the first edition, and to Andy Bulmer and Michal Sluzarczyk for their work on the second.

We took thousands of photographs to try and capture the atmosphere of Bettys. It was so difficult to choose which to use in this book, especially as so many customers were excited at the prospect of being included in this little piece of history. We are sorry to have disappointed so many.

For those who were caught on camera when they were supposed to be somewhere else,
our sincere apologies. We endeavoured to get everyone's permission.

Every effort has been made to trace the copyright holders of additional material used in this book. We thank Eden Camp, Ian Boyle Shipping, Marine Art Posters, DND Canada, Graham Hall Postcards, Theatre Museum, Crispin Hughes/Oxfam, Don Burluraux, Christine Shepherd, the ILN Picture Library, Unnetie Digital Archive, and the NRM/SSPL who have all provided additional memorabilia and other images. If anyone has been overlooked, we will acknowledge them in any future editions.

The final thank you is to Victor Wild.
I am convinced he still has a few secrets up his sleeve,
but that's for another volume.

*My father, Victor Wild,
in his greenhouse with his
coffee and cocoa plants*

We hope you have enjoyed this book. If you would like further copies
please visit www.bettys.co.uk or call in at one of our Bettys Café Tea Rooms:

Parliament Street, Harrogate

RHS Garden Harlow Carr, Harrogate

St Helen's Square, York

Stonegate, York

The Grove, Ilkley

High Street, Northallerton

If you think you know who Betty really is or have any anecdotes
or memorabilia for our archives, please write to me
at 1 Parliament Street, Harrogate HG1 2QU.
I look forward to hearing from you.